FIXING
URBAN
SCHOOLS

FIXING
URBAN
SCHOOLS

Paul T. Hill *and*
Mary Beth Celio

BROOKINGS INSTITUTION PRESS
Washington, D.C.

Copyright © 1998 by
THE BROOKINGS INSTITUTION
1775 Massachusetts Avenue, N.W., Washington, D.C. 20036

Library of Congress Cataloging-in-Publication data

Hill, Paul Thomas, 1943–
 Fixing urban schools / Paul T. Hill and Mary Beth Celio.
 p. cm.
 Includes bibliographical references and index.

 ISBN 0-8157-3613-4 (pbk. : permanent paper)
 1. Education, urban—United States. 2. School improvement
programs—United States. I. Celio, Mary Beth. II. Title.
 LC5131 .H46 1998
 370'.9173'2—ddc21

            98-25500
             CIP

9 8 7 6 5 4 3 2 1

The paper used in this publication meets minimum requirements
of the American National Standard for Information Sciences—Per-
manence of Paper for Printed Library Materials: ANSI Z39.48-1984.

Typeset in Minion

Composition by Cynthia Stock
Silver Spring, Maryland

Printed by Automated Graphic Systems
White Plains, Maryland

Foreword

IN MANY big cities, individuals and institutions outside the educational system are being asked to create rescue strategies for the public schools. In Cleveland and Chicago, mayors have taken control of the school system and are searching for ways to transform failed schools and raise student achievement across the board. In the District of Columbia, as in Baltimore, lay reform boards have been asked both to navigate a school system through its day-to-day crises and to create a new strategy that will substantially increase performance. These assignments to non-educators are desperate measures because successive school boards and superintendents in these and other cities have been unable to unite educators on an improvement strategy.

Today's mayors, civic and foundation leaders, and school boards must therefore construct new solutions. Like new management teams taking over troubled businesses, they must avoid being drawn into every issue that concerns people inside the system. They need to devise strategies that are sophisticated enough to raise the performance of a very complex organization, yet are simple enough to integrate the efforts of many people. This book is directed to them.

In 1996 Brookings created an urban education reform program designed to give city leaders a place to turn for help. This book, that program's first product, is based on a study of cause and effect in education reform. The study examined the reasoning behind proposals intended to transform urban school systems, including improving student performance standards, investing in teacher retraining and new designs for schools, decentralizing school systems, creating school charters and contracting out for schools, and instituting vouchers.

The study concluded that each of those proposals offers something important, but that none is strong enough to transform a struggling city school system on its own. The different reform proposals are potentially complementary. Together these proposals might become effective strategies. At present, however, combined strategies that draw from the strengths of different reform approaches are hindered by rivalries and ideological conflicts.

Directed toward city leaders—mayors, school board members, foundation heads, leaders of civic and cultural institutions, and members of professions other than K–12 education, *Fixing Urban Schools* distills four categories of lessons: how to start creating a citywide reform strategy; where to get help; how to construct a reform strategy that is bold enough to work; and how to put the strategy into action and make sure it works as expected. It concludes that effective big-city reform strategies are possible. But many things must change. Scholars who invent and advocate for reform ideas must adopt principles of truth-in-advocacy. Foundations and businesses that support local reform efforts must adopt the discipline of cause-and-effect thinking and refuse to be captured by ideas that are too one-sided to work. Local authorities must resist adopting feel-good and quick-fix reforms and commit to hard-nosed evaluation and continuous strengthening of reform initiatives.

The authors wish to thank the many people who endured their questions and provided materials and advice, including John Anderson, Brian Benzel, Louann Bierlein, Susan Bodilly, Anthony Bryk, Barbara Cervone, John Coons, Howard Fuller, Thomas Glennan, James Guthrie, Anne Hallett, Jane Hannaway, Frederick Hess, Michael Knapp, Ted Kolderie, Robert Litan, Thomas Loveless, Lorraine McDonnell, Milbrey McLaughlin, Linda McNeill, Terry Moe, Betty Jane Narver, Robert Palaich,

James Peyser, Lawrence Pierce, Eric Premack, Diane Ravitch, Lois Rice, Ronn Robinson, Cecelia Rouse, the late Donald Schon, Robert Schwartz, Ted Sizer, Marshall Smith, Carol Weiss, Priscilla Wohlstetter, and William Zumeta. They are also grateful to Christine Campbell, Robin Lake, and Kathleen Elliott Yinug for their help on all parts of the project. Deborah Styles edited the manuscript, while Paul Corrington indexed and Trish Weisman proofread the pages.

Brookings gratefully acknowledges the Alcoa Foundation, the Edna McConnell Clark Foundation, the Joyce Foundation, and the Pew Charitable Trusts for the financial support provided this project.

The views expressed in this volume are those of the authors and should not be ascribed to the organizations whose assistance is acknowledged above or to the trustees, officers, or other staff members of the Brookings Institution.

MICHAEL H. ARMACOST
President

August 1998
Washington, D.C.

Contents

Struggling to Improve City Schools 1

T HE HEAT is on urban public school systems. Since the mid-1980s, state legislatures, state education departments, and courts have dismantled local school boards and administrative structures. They have placed the schools in the hands of mayors, state officials, or specially appointed boards of local leaders. This has happened in Newark and Paterson, New Jersey, Cleveland, Chicago, Baltimore, and the District of Columbia. By the end of 1998 it might also happen in Philadelphia, Hartford, Connecticut, and other cities.

Takeovers by courts and state governments are intended to break political gridlock, lessen the iron grip of bureaucratic routine, and make room for people who might have new ideas. But, as one prominent mayor has said, "I had good intentions and some hunches, but no ideas about what to do or where to get help." Leaders newly placed in charge of struggling school systems have moved aggressively to improve fiscal controls, building maintenance, and personnel policies, but most have floundered in the search for ways to encourage better school performance.

In trying to improve the performance of their public schools, the leaders of big cities face problems of two kinds, intellectual and political. The

1

intellectual problem is the absence of a guiding philosophy for reform. The political problem is the difficulty of building and keeping a coalition strong enough to overcome the resistance to change that is endemic to a large organization whose constituency comprises contending interest groups and civil service employees. Few communities have had the benefit of both a strong set of ideas and a political support structure that lasted long enough to bring those ideas to fruition.

No one knows exactly how to solve all the problems of big-city public school systems. But it is obvious that the future of millions of young city dwellers, for whom the public schools are a necessary route to employability and membership in the broader society, is at stake.

This book is about where the people responsible for improving big-city school systems might start. It is addressed to lay leaders—to mayors, city council and school board members, heads of foundations and cultural institutions, and business leaders, all of whom are called on from time to time to consider what can be done about their cities' low-performing schools. It is also addressed to school superintendents and teacher leaders who are convinced that fundamental, strategy-driven change is necessary. For those audiences, the book tries to identify the essential elements of reform strategies that can transform school performance in big cities beset by poverty, social instability, racial isolation, and labor unrest. The book also suggests ways that local leaders can assemble the necessary political and administrative support to make such reforms work.

Superintendents Are Not Enough

Big-city school superintendents keep their jobs, on average, for three years. Once a superintendent leaves, the officials responsible for the school system search for and hire a new superintendent, usually a capable and experienced person who takes the job confident in his or her plan to improve the schools and raise student achievement. Three years later, on average, that person is gone, plans only partly implemented and goals unfulfilled. Then the process repeats itself.

Every now and then a superintendent stays long enough to implement a definite reform plan. Richard Wallace stayed long enough in Pittsburgh in the mid-1980s to put in place a highly structured curriculum that made sure low-income and minority students were taught basic skills. John Murphy stayed long enough in Prince George's County, Maryland, and Charlotte, North Carolina, to put in place a reform plan that held school principals strictly accountable for annual student improvement. This plan was based on carefully designed tests developed at the district level. Joseph Fernandez stayed long enough in Dade County, Florida, to devolve significant decisionmaking power to individual schools and institute a program that kept pace with rapidly growing school enrollment by creating focused, thematic new schools. In these and other comparable cases, the superintendent's reform plan began to bear fruit, manifested in improved school programs and slight but measurable increases in student test scores. In every case, however, when the superintendents left, their reform programs were dismantled or superseded.

Leadership transitions happen for many reasons—sometimes because the superintendent burns out or is offered a more exciting opportunity and sometimes because the superintendent's aggressive pursuit of a reform strategy has hurt too many feelings and stimulated too many complaints. For whatever reason, such transitions almost always send local community leaders back to square one, with no particular idea about how to reform the school system—other than to find someone whose ideas are a sharp departure from the previous superintendent's. On occasion school boards will select someone in their own system, an assistant or deputy superintendent, who has been groomed for the job. Such successors seldom have the charisma and political skill of their predecessors, so the reform strategy seldom continues in its original form.

There is much more to be said about the difficulties of reform in big-city school systems, but the point is clear: city leaders need more than new superintendents. They also need more than catchy slogans. City leaders have been told for too long that everything would be all right if only all adults came to believe that all children can learn. No city has yet been able to figure out how to translate that slogan into an effective plan of action. City leaders need permanent reform strategies strong enough to move an entrenched system. They desperately need ideas about how to reform the structures, incentives, and capacities of the public school system so that schools can be focused on instruction, teachers can teach effectively, and students can learn.

The "great man" and the "great slogan" theories do not work for city school systems. If a leader emerges with a strategy bold enough to make a difference, he or she is likely to be deposed by opponents or drawn away by another district that will pay almost anything to get someone who offers hope. When that happens, the leader's initiative, which depended almost entirely on one individual's energy and prestige, quickly collapses, and conditions return to the status quo ante.

Partly as a result of repeated searches for great men and too ready acceptance of slogans without specific content, big American cities have little to show for ten years of work on the problems of the public schools. Nearly half of all urban public school students are still giving up on schooling before they can read and write well enough to make a living with anything other than their hands.

Understanding the Problem

Efforts to reform big-city school systems have followed the pattern of incrementalism and fragmentation established by federal aid to education in the 1960s. Public education, as a government function run by civil servants and operating under rules made by political decisionmaking bodies, is assumed to have a sound structure and is therefore left alone. Funders, including federal and state governments, foundations, and businesses, identify particular groups of students to help or specific programs to support. Every school thus becomes host to many programs, each focused on a particular problem or beneficiary and each running autonomously as if nothing else were happening. These separate efforts compete for the time and attention of teachers, administrators, and students and often end up getting in each other's way. Many individuals and groups have good ideas, but no one person or group is able to pursue any line of action very far. That is why there can be many reform initiatives and little progress.

Big-city school systems like Los Angeles, New York, Chicago, and Milwaukee are trying to give individual schools more control over teaching methods while at the same time issuing new mandates for multicultural education, diversity training, AIDS awareness, and recognition of students' different learning styles. Some city systems are mounting several different teacher training programs simultaneously, some aimed at retraining teachers in subjects where many are deficient, others aimed at convincing teachers that the only valid knowledge is what they formulate for themselves and their own students. None of these programs or processes is necessarily bad in itself, but a school or school district that pursues all of them at once will not get the benefit of any.

Sources of Ideas for Fundamental Reform

After a decade of efforts to improve American public schools incrementally and from within, the initiative for education reform has shifted to those who propose far more radical measures. As a result, communities and states are now seriously debating reform options such as state takeovers, chartering private agencies to run schools, and private school voucher plans that would have been considered implausible only a few years ago. The defining features of the American public school system that came together after the Supreme Court's 1954 *Brown* decision— direct operation of schools by elected school boards, compliance-based accountability, civil service employment for teachers, mandatory assignment of students to schools, and control of funds by central district bureaucracies—are now under serious challenge.

Traditionally, efforts to improve public schools have focused on the technical aspects of teaching and learning—on new instructional materials, better tests, and new methods for teaching particular subjects. Such efforts made some schools marginally better, but they left intact the existing system of bureaucratic controls, group entitlements, and job protections. In the context of an essentially frozen system, such micro-scale changes have not been enough to reverse the disastrous decline of big-city school systems or to restore public confidence.[1] Middle-class families of all races (including the children of public school teachers) continue defecting to private schools. Polls reveal that 28 percent of Americans now give the public schools a grade of D or F (below average).[2] That percentage is up from 14 percent in 1987. Since 1991 more Americans have said the nation's public schools are below average than say they are above average, and the gap widens by the year. Partly as a result, the professional groups that have dominated public education since World War II —the teachers' unions, permanent state and local administrators, and the providers of special services to defined groups of children—have lost the initiative, on both political and intellectual fronts.

The initiative has shifted to people outside the mainstream of public education who have proposed more fundamental reforms. Starting with publication of *Politics, Markets, and America's Schools*, by John Chubb and Terry Moe,[3] analysts have proposed various initiatives intended to replace regulatory compliance with student performance standards, to make schools' existence and staff members' jobs contingent on performance, to give families choices among public schools, and to transfer control of public funds from centralized bureaucracies to individual schools. Such proposals are intended to rise above the confusion of many small efforts, to change systems rather than simply individuals or programs. Some of these proposals are outlined below.

Standards

Imposition of standards would establish clear expectations about what students are to be taught and to learn, setting high targets for student performance. Standards would allow for the creation of an aligned system of tests, curricula, teacher training, and teaching materials. They would attach real consequences to test results for schools, students, and individual teachers alike. Standards-based reform assumes that clarity about what must be taught and learned will create demand for improvements in educational methods, focus teacher effort on instruction, and motivate parents and students to strive for higher levels of performance. Students will learn because their goals will be clear and the efforts of adults in the schools will be focused on instruction.

Teacher Development

Reform based on teacher professional development assumes that teachers who take responsibility for their own learning and practice will become more effective in the classroom and that the spirit of innovation will engage teachers whose methods are now stagnant. It is also predicated on the idea that methods developed by teachers will be of higher quality than those created by nonteachers. Teacher excitement about improved practice, in turn, will drive reform of public school systems. Students will learn because their teachers will be energetic, well prepared, and engaging.

School Designs

Every school would be assigned to implement a comprehensive plan based on a particular approach to pedagogy. For example, a school might decide to base its approach on teaching through student-initiated projects, on computer-based instruction, or on the study and discussion of great books. Design-based reform assumes that schools that use a defined and consistent approach to instruction will be more focused and consistent, that teachers in such schools will work together more productively, and that parents and students will fully understand what the school promises and what is required of them. It also assumes that schools and districts will select and use effective designs for integrating whole schools around an approach to instruction. Students will learn because their schools are organized to provide consistent high-quality instruction and to remedy teaching and learning failures as they occur.

Decentralization and Site-Based Management

Decentralization that results in local (site-based) management will provide new decisionmaking roles for teachers and parents, often in conjunction with reduction of the size and powers of a local school system's central office. Decentralization-based reform assumes that greater school-level engagement in decisionmaking will encourage teachers and principals to take the initiative in rethinking their instructional methods and their relationships to families and neighborhoods. It also assumes that parents will become more engaged in their children's schooling. Teachers and parents will work together to overcome home and neighborhood factors that interfere with teaching and learning. Students will learn because their teachers know that effective instruction depends on them and because parents and neighbors, who understand and support the schools' efforts, will not tolerate lax performance by students or teachers.

Charter Schools

A limited number of schools would be authorized to operate independently as long as they got good results for students and abided by public sector rules on equity of student admission and fiscal accounting. Parents would be allowed to choose among schools. Charter schooling assumes that the opportunity to innovate will unite parents and teachers; that schools of choice will become strong communities; and that rivalry between charter schools and regular public schools will lead to demand for more widespread innovation and school freedom. Students will learn because schools will be specialized to meet particular needs and will strive to be considered highly effective.

School Contracting

School-specific performance agreements would be created. These would give schools complete control over their funds and staffing as long as they delivered the promised combination of curriculum and instructional methods. All families would be allowed to choose the schools their children attended. Contracting assumes that school independence and competition for students will encourage the search for more effective methods of instruction and that family choice will strengthen the schools and family-school bonds. Students will learn because competition will force every school to focus its work on an explicit theory of teaching and learning; parents will be able to select schools that match their children's interests and learning styles.

Vouchers

Direct public funding of schools would be eliminated in favor of giving parents vouchers that were redeemable for tuition at any school. Voucher proposals assume that plenty of demand will attract high-quality independent school providers and drive innovation and that choice will allow families to select schools that they trust and can support. Students will learn because competition will favor schools that are productive and responsive and will eliminate schools that provide ineffective instruction.

Each of these proposals addresses one or more negative aspects of the current public education system: standards attack the system's tolerance of mediocrity; professional development takes on inattention to teacher quality; new school designs are meant to unify schools; decentralization corrects for micromanagement by school boards and central offices; charters address the problems created by a bureaucratic monopoly's operation of schools; contracting counteracts the current absence of arrangements for holding schools accountable as units; and vouchers provide choices for parents where previously such choices were limited.

These are all plausible ideas, but they are certainly different from one another. A person new to the field might understand that each of the ideas is limited, but that combinations may be possible. A newcomer might also be surprised to learn that these ideas are seldom used in combination and that, in fact, the proponents of the different reform ideas often consider one another rivals, not collaborators.

Goals of This Study

The reform proposals just summarized are based on powerful ideas. However, bringing all the available ideas fully to bear on the problems of urban education requires an effort to sort out the competing claims of different reform promoters and to bridge the chasms dividing them.

Since 1996 Brookings has encouraged collaboration among reform theorists, scholars, and educators, with the goal of providing advice and assistance to city leaders searching for effective reform strategies. The project on which this book is based focused on the cause-and-effect assumptions underlying the reform proposals summarized earlier. We treated each of the reform proposals as an intervention meant to perturb an ongoing system with a goal of producing a definite result. For each of the system-changing reform proposals we asked:

—What exactly is the intervention?

—What will be the direct result of the intervention (what behaviors or capabilities will it directly change)?

—How will these direct effects translate into changes in schools (how will the intervention lead to changes in teacher capabilities and performance or to student effort and learning)?

We tried to answer these questions in two ways, first by reading the books and articles in which the main proponents of standards, teacher development, decentralization, school designs, charters, contracting, and vouchers explained their ideas and defended them against critics (see appendix B).

Second, we talked extensively with the proposals' originators and with state and local leaders who had tried to put the proposals into effect. We interviewed approximately thirty such people in person, by telephone, and in a workshop held at Brookings in February 1997. As we explained to respondents, "We hope you will take the question and run with it, explaining why you believe the initiative can work as intended, who the key actors are, what they must do, what obstacles they must overcome, and how you will know whether the effort is working. We would also like to know what you think is the nature of the evidence that leads you to believe the initiative can improve public education." We also asked respondents what they had learned or how they had amended their reform proposals since first formulating them.

To explain the inquiry further, we used graphic examples of cause-and-effect relationships. Many found the accompanying Rube Goldberg illustration useful—and painfully evocative of the problem of framing strategies than can plausibly move a system as complex and mysterious as public education. In the cartoon, the simple act of scratching the man's back is accomplished through a complex and apparently bizarre series of seemingly unrelated actions.

This book builds from data and analysis to recommendations. The next three chapters provide the evidence and thinking that lead to the recommendations outlined in chapter 5. Chapter 2 analyzes the cause-and-effect assumptions that underlie the system-changing reform proposals and examines the proposals' limitations. It concludes that the competing reform proposals are each too weak to transform a strug-

The Automatic Back Scratcher

Rube Goldberg™ and © of Rube Goldberg Inc. Distributed by United Media.

Flame from lamp (A) catches on curtain (B) and fire department sends stream of water (C) through window — Dwarf (D) thinks it is raining and reaches for umbrella (E), pulling string (F) and lifting end of platform (G) — iron ball (H) falls and pulls string (I), causing hammer (J) to hit plate of glass (K) — crash of glass wakes up pup (L) and mother dog (M) rocks him to sleep in cradle (N), causing attached wooden hand (O) to move up and down along your back.

gling urban school system, but that hybrid strategies combining the strengths of rival proposals could be much more powerful. Chapter 3 shows that rival reforms as different as vouchers and standards share important ideas about what makes a good school. It also explains why, despite this apparent consensus, rival reformers are reluctant to collaborate with one another. Chapter 4 explores the ideological hot buttons that now prevent collaboration among people who have potentially complementary ideas. It shows why local leaders should not be afraid to contemplate reform strategies that include elements of family choice and school competition and allow different schools to pursue a broad variety of educational strategies. Chapter 5 provides advice to lay leaders faced with the need to reform a struggling urban school system: how do they get started, how do they avoid getting overwhelmed by day-to-day pressures, and how do they develop strategies that can make a real difference? Chapter 6 summarizes Brookings plans for a long-term program of studies and assistance aimed to help big-city leaders build and put into effect comprehensive K–12 education reform strategies. Finally, appendix A presents materials for a table-top simulation that can help leaders practice creating reform strategies for a fictional city before they are faced with the need to create real strategies for their own cities.

How Different Reform Proposals Are Supposed to Work | 2

Serious people have suggested every one of the reform proposals summarized in chapter 1. Each of the proposals addresses a real problem in urban education—low standards, poorly prepared and demoralized teachers, scarcity of designs for schools that can help disadvantaged children learn as much as their more advantaged peers, school systems' resistance to new ideas, lack of parental choice, and absence of performance incentives.

However, some serious people have also rejected each of the reform proposals as unrealistic or insufficient. Proponents of one proposal typically reject and deride the others, and they can expect to have the favor returned. How can people think so differently about one very obvious problem? This chapter summarizes the results of our effort to find out. It summarizes the methods we used to clarify proponents' ideas about how their reforms would lead to school improvement and increases in student learning and analyzes the results.

Cause-and-Effect Analysis

As sources of information, we relied heavily on the people whose names are associated with the major reform proposals—those who originated or most publicly articulated the ideas and those who first tried to put them into practice. We read what they had written and interviewed them at length in pursuit of answers to two simple questions: how was the proposed initiative expected to lead to better teaching and learning, and what events and actions are necessary if the initiative is to work as expected? What had they learned that led them to amend or elaborate their reform proposals since first formulating them?[1]

Interviews were exhaustive, as we often asked our informants to reason both backward and forward—from their favored reform initiative all the way through the system of adult actions that led to changes in instruction and student learning, and from the student all the way back to the intervention. The latter exercise proved both difficult and fruitful, since many respondents had never before written down all they assumed must occur before their proposed initiatives led to real improvements in teaching and learning. We hoped to understand, as completely as possible from the point of view of the reform originators, what chains of events the reforms were expected to set off and how they were expected ultimately to benefit children.

From the results of this research we created a complex cause-and-effect diagram for every reform, showing all the events that the originators assumed would lead from the proposed reform initiative to student learning and school improvement. However, aside from probing the reformers' logic and experience, we did not ask for empirical proof that the proposal was actually working as expected. Our results, then, amount to a best-case analysis of the individual reform proposals.

This mode of analysis is not easy on the reform originators. Asking them to trace a chain of actions from a proposed initiative to its final consequences erects a higher standard than most reform proposals have previously been subject to. It forces identification of hidden assumptions and poorly grounded expectations, among them the hope that once people see how good an idea is they will all adopt it. The more common standard is plausibility: is the proposed action plausibly related to school improvement?

In urban public education, where so little is working well, many initiatives can meet a standard of plausibility. That is why in many cities there are often many competing, small, plausible, ultimately ineffective reform efforts. When schools are run down and have poor equipment, spending more money is plausible. When many teachers are poorly educated and have weak control of their subjects or instructional technique, teacher training initiatives are plausible. When pupils get good grades without learning the material normally expected for students of their age, raising academic standards is plausible. When teachers and principals suffer low morale and feel burdened by bureaucracy, efforts to give them control over school decisions are plausible. When parents feel alienated from the schools, giving them choices among schools is plausible. However, such plausible initiatives are often ineffective. They may not work because the politics of jobs and patronage continues to divert extra money into hiring, unmotivated teachers neglect training opportunities, weak schools treat standards as unnecessarily high, bureaucracies continually thwart school initiatives, and parents find they have no good choices available.

Many proposals sound good. They might, despite their limitations, become vital parts of a broader strategy. This is true of many narrower-gauge proposals such as those typically pursued by school districts and their business supporters—buying computers, giving teachers a half-day each week to plan collaboratively, paying for teachers to take graduate courses, creating parent advisory groups, hiring adult members of minority communities to work in classrooms, buying new books and materials. Some of these initiatives have had localized successes and have contributed to measurable improvements in a few schools. However, as initiatives to improve large numbers of schools or whole school systems, none has been successful: outside the few schools under the direct influence of the reform originators, such initiatives have encountered other factors that neutralize or overcome them.

This distinction between a fully developed causal analysis and an assertion of plausibility helps explain education reformers' concern with the problem of scaling up. As Richard Elmore and others have noted, many promising proposals flourish in one or two schools or among groups of enthusiasts, but they do not survive when they are applied on a larger scale.[2] These initiatives are plausible, and they can have the desired effects in situations where their originators can control all relevant factors. However, outside hothouse conditions, the initiatives are watered down or are defeated by factors beyond their originators' control.

Thus the initiatives themselves are causally incomplete—they are plausible, but they do not specify the most important factors that will determine their success. Causal analysis sets a higher standard than mere plausibility: it starts by asking whether a proposal makes logical sense, but then it asks harder questions about whether the proposed actions are likely to set off a chain of complementary actions that lead to the desired result.

Given the history of the past ten years of education reform, it should not be unexpected that our study revealed that none of these proposals is, in itself, powerful enough or well enough thought through to transform our entrenched, mediocre city school systems. This conclusion certainly did not surprise the originators of the reform proposals, who understand how strongly the system resists change. However, reformers from different camps are often reluctant to acknowledge the limitations of their ideas and to accept the need for broader reform strategies combining the strengths of competing approaches.

Paradigm for Causal Analysis

We tried tracing the reform originators' theories from the immediate actions they proposed all the way to the hoped-for ultimate effects on student learning. To do this, we planned to organize the reformers' theories into two zones and a target (see figure 2-1). The reform initiative itself—for example, giving parents vouchers or creating a set of new school designs—is external. Inside the figure is the student, whose education the reform initiative is supposed to improve.[3] Between the initiative and the student are a yellow zone, encompassing the expected responses by the main actors and institutions in the public education system to the reform initiatives (for instance, parents who get vouchers search for schools; schools try to attract parents to get their vouchers), and a red zone, comprising the resulting changes in the student's immediate learning environment that might potentially affect student learning.

As we laid out the cause-and-effect assumptions beneath each of the reform proposals, we found our red and yellow zones were insufficient. There was a third zone in every theory, the blue zone, represented by the

Figure 2-1. *Paradigm for Cause and Effect of Reform Initiatives*

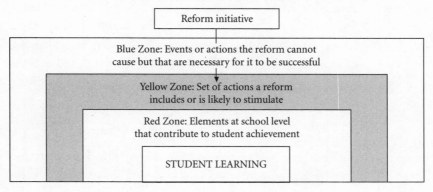

outer shell of figure 2-1. This zone contains the actions and events that the reform initiative cannot cause but which the reform initiators agree must occur if schools and student learning are to improve.

The blue zone, which our respondents and interviewers came to call the "zone of wishful thinking," might be the most important discovery of this study. The existence of a zone of wishful thinking in every major reform proposal means that none of them has clearly articulated where it falls short and none has all the ingredients necessary to improve teaching and learning through a public education system. This is true even in the best case, taking the reform originators' cause-and-effect assumptions as given.

Causal Models and Zones of Wishful Thinking

Figure 2-2 illustrates the different zones for one reform proposal, public school contracting, with arrows indicating the anticipated connections. This is our own proposal, and we feel confident that we have represented it fairly.[4] As the figure shows, educational contracting is supposed to set off a complex sequence of events, leading in the red zone to teacher collaboration and increased parental interest in and support for education. Clearly, contracting has a zone of wishful thinking. Several key actors must develop capabilities and patterns of action that they do not have

Figure 2-2. A Causal Model for Educational Contracting

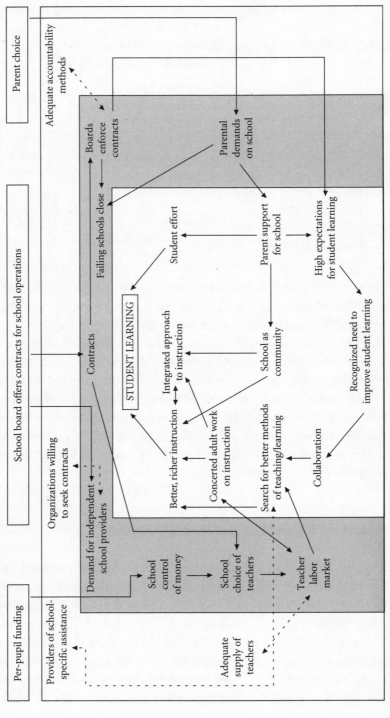

now. Contracting might create necessary preconditions for these developments, but it will not directly cause them. For example:

—Private organizations must be willing to accept contracts to operate schools;

—Organizations that have not previously run public schools must learn how to do so effectively;

—There must be an adequate supply of teachers willing and able to work without civil service protection in schools whose existence depends on performance;

—Parents must learn how to exercise informed choices among alternative contract schools; and

—Public authorities—superintendents and school board members—must find ways to hold individual schools accountable for the value they add to students' knowledge, not for what students knew before they entered the school.

Two other proposals, charter schools and education vouchers, have similar blue zones. Both assume, for example, a massive response of new suppliers wanting to run schools, an adequate supply of teachers who will be willing and able to cope with the demands of working in an environment of competition and strict performance accountability, and public authorities who learn how to protect students against low-quality schools or inequitable admissions processes without interfering with schools' ability to pursue coherent instructional programs. The voucher proposal also makes an assumption that contracting and charter proposals do not: that entrepreneurs will spontaneously offer good schools in poverty areas where teaching can be difficult and parents are less demanding.[5]

There is no reason in theory why the actions and events in contracting's zone of wishful thinking cannot take place. But they require actions and capabilities that are extremely rare today. Much the same is true for the other reform initiatives we studied. None of them causes all of the changes in public education necessary to achieve the results they aspire to. All have major zones of wishful thinking.

For example, the standards proposal calls for clear student performance requirements, testing to determine whether students meet the standards, and administration of rewards and penalties to schools, students, and individual teachers, depending on test results. Standards' yellow zone, the set of actions that a standards initiative includes or is likely to stimulate, includes government-funded efforts to construct standards for learning in every discipline, to create curricula and teaching techniques aligned to particular standards, and to retrain teachers who do not know how to present material effectively. Like contracting, standards has an important zone of wishful thinking. It assumes, for example, that

—State and local officials will release schools from regulatory restraints that impede school-level innovation and problem-solving;

—Teachers' and other unions will drop or renegotiate contracts that prevent response to new standards;

—Teachers and others who participate in standards-creating processes will be able to constrain others who advocate for individual disciplines from establishing requirements that are counterproductive and, in the aggregate, exceed any school's capabilities;

—Assistance providers will arise to help teachers learn how to meet standards that few existing schools now meet;

—Schools will find ways to blend the separate standards constructed for each discipline into a coherent overall instructional program; and

—Schools and teachers whose students fall far below standards will strive to meet them rather than defining them as unrealistic and therefore irrelevant.

Recognizing these limitations, some standards supporters have formulated a more ambitious reform strategy, called *systemic reform*, which postulates that states will align the entire public education system—standards, testing, curriculum, instructional methods, allocation of funds, preservice teacher training, in-service teacher training, principal training and selection, parent participation, rewards and penalties for educators and students, employers' hiring standards, and higher education admissions requirements—to reinforce standards. According to supporters, systemic reform is an idea that fits a need perfectly: if all these aspects of the education and work system could be perfectly aligned, standards would surely drive public education. However, like a perpetual motion machine, systemic reform assumes away the very natural phenomena that must be overcome: state legislatures are inherently fractious and inconsistent, educators and parents cannot all be persuaded that there is a single all-important set of facts and skills that all students must master, and employers and higher education institutions constantly revise their standards in response to developments in the economy, technology, arts, and sciences. Rather than eliminating standards' zone of wishful thinking, systemic reform multiplies the number and complexity of events that must occur but that the reform proposal itself cannot cause.

A final example of a proposal with an important blue zone, school system decentralization, calls for deregulating public schools and increasing the scope of decisions that can be made by combinations of school-site administrators, teachers, and parents. Decentralization's yellow zone (the set of actions that a decentralization initiative includes or is likely to stimulate) includes schools seeking waivers from burdensome rules, increased parental activism, and a restructuring of teacher and principal roles to emphasize problem solving over compliance. Elements of decentralization's zone of wishful thinking include assumptions that

—School system central offices will adopt the spirit of decentralization and forbear from making new rules and enforcing existing ones that reduce school autonomy;

—School communities that are diverse and not accustomed to shared decisionmaking will find ways to collaborate effectively on school improvement;

—Tenured teachers and their unions will agree to instructional changes desired by parents and other community members; and

—Superintendents and school boards will find ways of holding schools accountable for student performance without eliminating schools' freedom of action.

Recognizing these limitations, leaders in communities that have tried decentralization have alloyed pure decentralization plans with elements of centralized control and assistance, including hiring private contractors to provide some services previously provided by bureaucratic agencies, school inspectors, advisors to struggling community groups, and authorities able to disband and reconstitute failed schools.[6] However, as with standards, modifications to the original reform strategy can introduce their own complexities, expanding rather than shrinking the reform's zone of wishful thinking. Thus the analysis that follows will present the unalloyed reforms as originally proposed.

Table 2-1. *The Zone of Wishful Thinking*

Reform theory	Events that the reform needs but cannot cause
Professional development/ teacher networks	School freedom to use new ideas Acceptance of new ideas by teachers not involved in original deliberations Parent acceptance of teacher-created ideas Public accountability systems that accept diverse student performance measures
Vouchers	Competent organizations willing to run schools Adequate supply of teachers willing to work in competitive environments Valid and readily available parent information Parental diligence in choosing schools Mechanisms to guarantee supply of good schools in areas serving less-demanding parents
Standards	School freedom to change Whole-school models that meet all standards Aligned investments in staff development Teacher acceptance of instructional changes Sanctions and capacity to reconstitute failed schools
School designs (New American Schools)	Freedom for schools to adopt designs School control of funds Public accountability systems that accept diverse student performance measures Teacher and parent acceptance of the idea of coherent schools with defined missions
Decentralization	Accountability system for individual schools Reduction of central office controls New and diverse sources of help for struggling schools Capacity to reconstitute failed schools
Charters	Accountability system for individual schools Large numbers of competent school providers School start-up assistance Appropriate training for school leaders and staff
Contracting	Accountability system for individual schools Large numbers of competent organizations willing to seek contracts Adequate supply of teachers willing to work under conditions of contracting Providers of school-specific assistance and training and parent information

Table 2-1 lists each of the reform ideas and a sample of elements of their "zones of wishful thinking."

Untapped Complementarities

A surprising discovery that emerged from our comparison of the cause-and-effect assumptions of different reform proposals was their potential complementarity.

As table 2-2 shows, some reform proposals are specifically designed to cause the events that are found in other proposals' zones of wishful thinking. For example, setting standards for what children should learn gives schools targets, but it does not show how the learning activities required to help students attain these standards can be woven together into a coherent plan for a whole school.[7] School designs can fill standards' zone of wishful thinking by providing plans for making all parts of a school work together to enhance student learning. However, despite

Table 2-2. *What One Reform Lacks Is Often Provided by Another*

Reform	Yellow zone (direct effects)	Blue zone (necessary conditions)
Networks	Teacher learning opportunities	Ways of reaching unmotivated teachers
Vouchers	Ways of reaching unmotivated teachers	New school providers
Standards	Clear expectations for learning, accountability	Whole-school models of practice
School designs	Whole-school models of practice	School freedom, control of funds and staff
Decentralization	Parent and teacher involvement	Ways to transform schools that do not change on their own
Charters	School freedom, control of funds and staff	Clear expectations for learning, accountability
Contracting	Ways to transform schools that do not improve on their own	Supply of teachers for a labor market

their obvious complementarity, the standards and school design proposals are often regarded as competing alternatives. Though some communities (such as Chicago, Memphis, Cincinnati, and San Antonio)[8] have started trying to exploit the complementary strengths of the two approaches, many standards advocates have attacked the school design movement as an unnecessary infringement on educators' freedom. What could be mutually supportive reforms are thus pitted against each other, to the detriment of both.

The situation of teacher development–based reforms is even more telling. Teacher development activities (retraining, networking) have strong effects on the teachers who participate in them voluntarily because of their tastes for or belief in such activities. But, as Elmore and others have pointed out, other teachers seldom accept or imitate the results of teacher development processes that they themselves did not choose to join. For this reason teacher development clearly needs some mechanism to influence people outside the immediate circle of its founding enthusiasts. Such a mechanism, which is in the zone of wishful thinking for teacher development, can be directly supplied by reforms like contracting, which put schools into competition with one another and therefore give teachers in a particular school a strong incentive to search for effective instructional methods and ensure that their actions complement one another.

Reforms based on increasing educators' knowledge and competence can also fill the zones of wishful thinking for incentive-based reforms like contracting and vouchers. The latter group of proposals assumes that better instructional methods, more competent teachers, and new organizations able to provide good schools in a demanding market environment will all appear spontaneously in response to incentives. Teacher development, standards, and new school designs can, at least in theory, help create needed capabilities that the incentive-based reforms can only wish into being.

Conclusion

This analysis does not prove that rival reforms can be force-fit together. The exact form of school competition that might best encourage reluctant teachers to take their professional development opportunities seriously must be thought through carefully. Similarly, a proper match of the school design idea with a charter-like arrangement—maximizing individual schools' incentives and opportunities to adopt coherent improvement strategies—requires considerable analysis.[9] As the next chapter shows, merging of reform proposals to maximize their combined strength requires social and political action to overcome ideological and political barriers that divide different education reform camps.

Agreements and Disagreements on How Reforms Work 3

IN LIGHT of the many fundamental differences among the reform proposals discussed above, we were surprised to discover how similar were the contending parties' ideas about how reforms of the system should affect schools and students. Even though they often used different vocabularies to describe their goals, all of the reform theorists whom we interviewed claimed that at a minimum their proposals would strengthen schools as institutions, promote serious adult collaboration, foster coherency in schools' instructional programs, and strengthen communal bonds between families and teachers. We found these similarities surprising in light of the drastically different angles from which different reform theorists would promote change. So did many of the reform theorists, many of whom regard one another as dedicated rivals with nothing in common.

This chapter explores the strange coexistence of harsh disagreements about the ways in which public education should change, with apparent agreement about the attributes of a good school and how school changes can lead to increased student learning. How can people who propose reform initiatives as unlike as vouchers—which would introduce competition and entrepreneurial control into public education—and teacher retraining—which presumes continuation of the existing government-run, civil service–manned system—agree on what should happen within schools? Is this agreement more apparent than real? Does it mask profoundly different views about the meaning of key processes like community building and adult collaboration?

Points of Agreement

All of the reform proposals discussed in the previous chapters are reactions to the failure of government, foundation, and business efforts to improve schools by creating regulations to guide action and providing marginal additions of money and other forms of assistance. Such efforts have generally failed, in part because the conditions of children and families in big cities have become worse faster than funding increased, and in part because regulations and the ways extra money has been used have made schools weaker. City schools have become holding companies for externally funded programs. As the numbers of external funders increase, the schools become more and more chaotic. City children, whose own lives are turbulent and unfocused, often attend schools where no two adults have the same ideas of what students are supposed to experience and where there are so many rules to follow that no adult feels any real control over or responsibility for what children learn. Some schools rise above this norm, but they are beset by a system that constantly micromanages and imposes new rules.[1]

Our research made it clear that the reform proposals all intend to make urban schools simpler, more focused places where adults share a set of ideas about what constitutes good teaching and where teachers and parents share responsibility for children's learning and well-being. This set of common elements, which reflects the many years of research on effective schools, is displayed in figure 3-1. Virtually all reformers agree that city schools must become places that teach to high standards, demand serious work and high performance from students and teachers alike, continually search for better teaching methods, unite the efforts of all adults, gain parents' confidence, and use parental support to motivate student work.

Figure 3-1. *The Model of Within-School Processes Shared by Most Reformers*

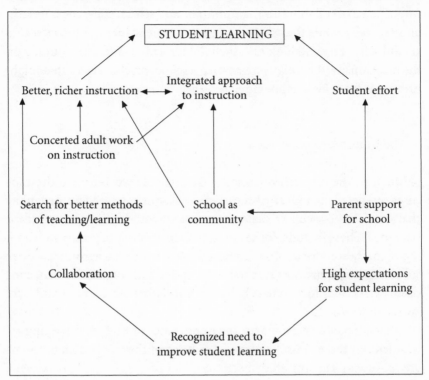

Figure 3-1 shows how these elements are supposed to work together to improve student learning. We constructed it in the course of our interviews with originators of the rival reform proposals, as it became clear that people were using different languages to describe a remarkably consistent picture of the good school. Every proposal, from teacher retraining to vouchers, identified the same set of critical aspects of school improvement and assumed they would interact in much the same way, even if they might not have drawn arrows in precisely the same directions.

How can this be? There are two answers, one emphasizing apparent agreement on goals and the other pointing out underlying disagreements. First, virtually all reform theorists are influenced by the same literature about factors contributing to successful schools: people agree about the importance of collaboration, community, and school coherency. Second, and crucially, while they share a common understanding of what a successful school should look like, the rival reformers differ profoundly on the mechanisms that might create such a school or, conversely, that might prevent it from ever happening.

The Common Background

Much of the research on what makes schools work for children focuses on specific school attributes. Different studies have identified many characteristics of schools that are correlated with high rates of student learning.[2] These include, for example, small school size, personalization, high expectations for all students regardless of family background, teacher collaboration, aggressive leadership, simplicity of the curriculum, consistent standards for student behavior and effort, and family and peer group support.[3]

There is a good rationale for the importance of each of these characteristics, but there is also evidence that none of them is sufficient to improve student learning all by itself.[4]

—Small schools allow faculty to know one another personally and to collaborate outside the big-school compartments of grade level and academic discipline. Small size also allows the principal to know every teacher and every student.

—Personalization, sometimes a consequence of small size, means that adults pay attention to the needs and development of every student and prevent emotional crises and learning plateaus from becoming serious problems.

—High expectations for all students lead faculty to regard a student's learning difficulties as a problem to be solved, not evidence of a permanent incapacity.

—Teacher collaboration implies that teachers coordinate their instruction so that students accumulate knowledge and understanding from course to course, and that teachers share responsibility for students' overall development.

—Aggressive school leadership focuses adult attention on the school's overall goals and fosters constant self-criticism, so that teachers do not assume that routines that worked for students in the past will also work today.

—Simple curricula focus the faculty's attention on a relatively small number of subjects, drawing all students toward learning a common core of challenging subjects.

—Consistent high standards for student behavior both inside and outside the school signal the school's commitment to learning and protects students from disruption by (and the temptation to disrupt) their peers. Such standards also eliminate corrosive doubts about the school's fairness toward students from different social classes and ethnic groups.

—Family support for the school ensures that parents will provide opportunities for homework and reinforce the school's demands on student time and attention.

—Supportive peer groups, which schools can foster at least in part by providing extracurricular opportunities and maintaining high standards for student behavior, weaken anti-school forces in the cool youth culture.

Some of the reform theorists we interviewed went beyond naming these individual school characteristics to endorsing a shared if weakly articulated theory of how the characteristics work together to make a good school. In our discussions with reform theorists, and subsequently in a separate research project, the authors have tried to clarify and explicate the underlying theory of the good school. The theory of integrative capital holds that the individual attributes identified by previous studies of school effectiveness are caused, unified, and sustained by something deeper.[5] That something deeper, integrative capital, is the set of ideas that unify the school—ideas about what students should learn, what specific experiences the school must arrange for students, and how the school must organize the work of teachers and other adults to ensure that students have those experiences.

A school's integrative capital is a unifying vision that establishes

—What ideas, facts, and habits the school intends to help students learn;

—What learning experiences the school intends to offer students and how it intends to provide those experiences in order to ensure that students do learn;

—What students the school intends to serve (defined by age groups, previous education, and other characteristics); and

—How the school will relate to those children's parents and the public officials responsible to act in the children's interests.[6]

Integrative capital is the educational analog of corporate strategy. For a business, corporate strategy is the unifying vision that holds together the work of the many disciplines that must collaborate if the firm is to succeed. Corporate strategy includes a definition of the product or service the firm intends to offer for sale; the firm's methods of product development and production; and its relationships with customers and suppliers.

People who visit many schools know that some are unified, disciplined, and consistent in what they expect of adults and offer students, and others are not. Unified schools are different from one another in many ways: some are private and some public; some are in rich neighborhoods and some in poor; and some use modern technology and up-to date instructional methods, while others are old-fashioned. What they have in common is integrative capital.

Schools that expect to make a major difference in what children know and can do have very clear goals, and they have definite methods of pursuing those goals. Those goals and methods color every transaction among faculty members and between faculty, students, parents, and other constituencies. Schools with integrative capital have definite approaches to motivating students, ensuring that learning is cumulative over time, and quickly identifying and helping students who begin to fall behind. Such schools also know exactly what they expect of their faculty. Though they expect faculty members to collaborate and solve problems, they do not expect teachers to operate as totally autonomous professionals. Leaders in such schools are respected as interpreters of the ideas that unite the school, but few rule through force of personality or base their authority on their formal legal status.

Weak and less coherent schools are hesitant to impose expectations that might conflict with home and neighborhood cultures that middle-class teachers only dimly understand. These schools are often diffident and readily abandon expectations that students or interest group representatives object to. Most are reluctant to engage topics that can become controversial and often content themselves with formulaic celebrations of ethnic and cultural customs. Stronger, more coherent schools regard diversity as a topic of respectful but serious conversation, not a source of distinctive rights. They do not translate differences in student background into differences in expectations for learning, effort, or behavior.

The conclusion that what productive schools have in common is coherency, clarity of purpose, and consistency of effort is not absolutely proven and might not be recognized or accepted by every reformer who otherwise agrees in principle on the characteristics of an effective school.[7] There has been no experiment that created schools high and low in integrative capital and compared their effectiveness. However, the conclusion meets two important tests of a scientific proposition: it is consistent with the existing data, and it explains the relationship between phenomena that were previously thought unrelated.

This agreement among reformers on the importance of school coherency—which we have called integrative capital—reflects a remarkable convergence on an image of the kind of school that should result from a reform initiative. Why, despite this apparently powerful agreement on the desired results of reform initiatives, can reformers differ so profoundly on how these results can be brought about?

Roots of Disagreement

We think there are three related but different reasons why people who agree on the desired results of urban reform initiatives still disagree so profoundly on how the desired changes in schools should be created:

—Reformers have profoundly different views, based on disciplinary and ideological divisions, about what motivates and disciplines adults to work productively on behalf of children.

—Reformers have conflicting basic assumptions, especially with regard to ideas about the roles of government and the private sector, and different hopes for distribution of income and opportunity among adults in society.

—Reformers do not agree on their assessment of the political and legal feasibility of different changes.

Disciplinary and Ideological Divisions

While the reform proposals agree in general about events that promote student learning, they divide on how the necessary conditions come about. As we discovered, the originators of different reform proposals are deeply divided on what can cause schools to take on vital characteristics (community, collaboration, parental support).

One set of reform advocates assumes that adults are motivated toward the actions that make schools effective almost entirely by *intrinsic* factors—by individual beliefs, fervor, dedication, and the inherent attractiveness of good ideas. Their reforms try to bring about better schools by informing and inspiring adults. Rival proposals rely almost entirely on *extrinsic* factors—on rules and regulations, financial incentives, and fear of lost employment. These reforms try to bring about better schools by motivating people to search for more effective methods, to cooperate because they understand that all staff members are equally at risk if the school fails, and to work hard. They do not rely on the intrinsic attractiveness of an idea or assume that moral commitment or inspiration are sufficient drivers for improvement.

Proponents of reforms emphasizing intrinsic factors are overwhelmingly persons dedicated to the education profession, deeply respectful of teachers and solicitous about their job security and satisfaction. They are confident of the moral superiority of schools as a public enterprise, free of commercial or economic motivations.

Supporters of reforms emphasizing extrinsic factors are overwhelmingly persons who do not make their living in public education and consider public bureaucracies inefficient—economists, political scientists, other professionals, and business managers. They think that choices made through political process are seldom as wise or efficient as private choices. Many are also openly hostile to government bureaucracies and civil service unions.

Differences between reforms relying on intrinsic and extrinsic motivation are illustrated in figure 3-2. For example, although all the reform proposals agree that teacher collaboration and adult community are necessary attributes of an effective school, they differ on how these attributes come about. Proponents of reforms based on intrinsic factors (for ex-

Figure 3-2. *How Intrinsic and Extrinsic Theories Differ on What Causes Critical Elements of Effective Schooling and Improved Student Learning*

Intrinsic cause or	Extrinsic cause	Leads to
Inspiration and conversion	Labor market and parent choice pressures	Concerted adult work on instruction
Consensus through deliberation	Recruitment to prior idea	Integrated approach to instruction
Professional or community standards	Competitive performance or consumer demand	High expectations for student learning
Voluntary networks and training for knowledge construction	Theorists, vendors, or design teams	Search for better method of teaching and learning
Parental participation in deliberative process	Parental choice	Parent support for school

ample, teacher development) think collaboration and community come from deliberation—consensus formation via sharing of visions and mutual conversion. Proponents of reforms based on extrinsic factors (such as vouchers and contracting) think collaboration is motivated by the need to attract students in a competitive market and that community is built by recruiting teachers and parents who share a common interest in a type of schooling. The intrinsic-extrinsic schools of thought divide in similar ways about what causes family support for a school and what leads to student effort, and on why teachers work to develop improved instructional methods.

Some reform proposals have mixtures of intrinsic and extrinsic elements. For example, charter proponents hope schools will attract groups of parents who share a taste for decisionmaking through deliberation. However, none of the major reform proposals we studied is deliberately grounded in a rigorous effort to combine the strengths of different approaches or to compensate for the weakness of one reform initiative with the strengths of others.

To business and community leaders and others who do not make their living in public education, the idea that an enterprise could be reformed without a combination of intrinsic and extrinsic factors would seem implausible. However, that is exactly what many of the reform proposals we have studied try to do. The authors of at least one reform proposal, vouchers, have frankly advertised it as a panacea. At the extremes, some reform initiators seriously think that teacher collaboration alone can lead to the reform of the whole public education system, while others seriously propose that all that is required is a change in the rules and incentives under which schools operate.

Why do potentially complementary reform movements remain separate? The answers are both ideological and economic. Reform proponents also separate themselves into armed camps because it can pay to do so. People with one-sided "extrinsic" proposals can capture media attention, book sales, and foundation grants. People with "intrinsic" agendas can count on the support of school bureaucracies, teachers' unions, and businesses and foundations eager to avoid controversy and be seen to do good. Similarly, political leaders and private funders can benefit from stories about individual student or teacher successes, whether or not these successes are isolated or short-lived.

People who advance intrinsic theories are typically educators, who selected education as a profession because they believe in the power of knowledge and commitment. People who advance extrinsic theories such as contracting and vouchers are typically not educators but political and economic analysts accustomed to thinking about systems of pressures and incentives.

These differences are ultimately ideological and cultural. Proponents of intrinsic theories often believe that strong and just school communities are founded on professional values and collective deliberation and that extrinsic reforms would weaken community by emphasizing competition and individualism. Proponents of extrinsic reforms believe that public sector deliberation creates ineffective enterprises and puts the interests of school employees and pressure groups above the needs of children. Both groups think they own the moral high ground and that proposals competing with their own would have disastrous consequences.

These differences, based as they are on ideology and moralized reasoning, can be harsh and profound. They can make reformers unwilling to deal seriously with one another, and they can lead to sharp and polemical debates.

Basic Assumptions about the Role of Government

Reformers differ profoundly on what groups of adults should provide public schools and what sorts of economic opportunities public education should provide for adults.

Perhaps the deepest fissure among reformers is between, on the one hand, those who distrust public bureaucracies and believe civil service employment is an inefficient constraint on schools and, on the other hand, those who trust such government-style arrangements and believe that the profit motive contaminates services provided by nongovernmental agencies. The writings of John Chubb and Terry Moe on vouchers typify the antigovernmental group that occupies one side of the ideological fissure.[8] They argue that public decisionmaking leads to unproductive overregulation and that public school boards have no incentive to resist teacher union demands that limit the capacity of school leaders to coordinate teachers' work and maintain school coherency. To the same end, others have argued that teacher unionization and civil service employment ensure that school funds will be disproportionately spent for teachers' salaries and benefits (and that other aspects of schooling—books, building maintenance, curriculum development, evaluation, and in-service training are thereby slighted).[9]

We must make clear that some of our own earlier writings place us in this camp. The case for educational contracting presented in *Reinventing Public Education* includes some of the arguments summarized above.[10] We have also argued, on the basis of our research on schools' integrative capital, that many of the impediments to school coherency are grounded in state laws and local public policies that structure and regulate schools. Most public schools are now products of geological layers of regulations, half-implemented reform initiatives, and bargains among adults. These structures promote isolation of parts of the school from one another, and their cumulative effect, when seen across a school, is fragmentation. There are three kinds of impediments to schools' gaining and keeping integrative capital: structural features of public education systems that make it difficult for schools to control their resources and activities; political impediments that make it difficult for public schools to choose and maintain a consistent line of action; and attitudinal impediments that make it difficult for people who have become accustomed to working in a public education environment to create or maintain coherent schools even when they have the opportunity to do so.

On the other side of the ideological divide are many reformers who believe that only publicly controlled schools can act in the public interest. Again, the debate is most vivid in connection with Chubb and Moe's voucher proposal.[11] Critics have argued that eliminating detailed political oversight and civil service staffing of schools will open up schools to separatist agendas and risk social fragmentation,[12] allow profit-seeking entrepreneurs to gull unsophisticated parents into choosing inferior schools,[13] allow school operators to pursue discriminatory admissions policies that ignore social objectives like racial integration, create adverse working environments, reduce pay for teachers, and allow windfall profits at the expense of school quality.

These claims and counterclaims beg for empirical test, but little evidence is available. Resistance to nongovernmental school provision has been so strong that few serious trials have been possible. Small-scale initiatives—like the private voucher programs in Milwaukee and New York and the state charter school laws that have given rise to nearly 800 privately run public schools nationwide—have not provided answers to all the questions. Results to date on issues such as race and class integration and profit skimming do not confirm opponents' fears. But, as subsequent chapters will suggest, the values and perspectives underlying these conflicts are too deep to be resolved by fragmentary evidence.

The politics of jobs exacerbates these conflicts. Defenders of government control and civil service employment note that public school systems have become the principal employers of African American and immigrant middle-class professionals in big cities.[14] Others associate public employment with growth in affirmative action and protections against sexual harassment and job discrimination. People who emphasize these public policy goals, which are distinct from the more direct educational objectives of school quality and student learning, fear initiatives that weaken governmental and civil service leverage on schools (for instance, vouchers, charters, contracting and, in some cases, standards).[15]

On the other side of the jobs issue, critics of civil service hiring also think that competitive private enterprise is inherently more productive and that a degree of teacher job insecurity is desirable. Some also hope to attract new groups of providers into public education—middle-class professionals of all races who have felt cut out of public education, managers who might be attracted to running schools that control their own budgets, able former teachers who quit because they could not tolerate public school rules and working conditions, alternative groups of urban minority adults (such as former military technicians, trainers, and officers), and small businesses that might compete with central office monopolies on school maintenance, supplies, after-school programs, and in-service training for teachers. Proponents of vouchers, charters, and contracting do not expect or intend their initiatives to drive minorities out of public education, but they are willing to contemplate the possibility of some substitution of former civil servants for others who will work differently.

Again no one knows what the jobs consequences of different reforms will be, because political opposition has prevented their being tried on any large scale. Supporters of vouchers and other initiatives that would drastically alter the supply arrangements for public education assume that the majority of teaching jobs will be filled by people who are now teaching. However, they do expect substantial turnover on the margins, and they do anticipate drastic reductions in spending and employment in the central offices of local school systems.[16]

Legal and Political Feasibility

Many people who think urban public education must change are nonetheless skeptical about the political feasibility of some of the most ambitious reform proposals. They note that the system has so far been able to resist or drastically limit the scope of reform initiatives such as contracting, charters, and vouchers. Based on some of the issues outlined immediately above, some would-be reformers steer clear of promoting changes that they fear would elicit strong opposition. Some also advocate less threatening reforms like standards, acknowledging that some elements of charter and contract schooling might ultimately be necessary if standards are to have all the desired effects.[17]

There are foundations for these concerns. Voucher, charter, and contract proposals all require explicit changes in state laws, especially those governing local school board authorities and collective bargaining for teachers. Efforts to change state legal frameworks via charter school laws have succeeded in more than half the states, but the laws enacted typically set low ceilings on the numbers of schools allowed and dilute school autonomy. No state has enacted a widely applicable voucher law, and even relatively modest pilot programs are usually challenged in court under state constitutional mandates for a "free and uniform system of public education."

Others are more optimistic that state-level legal and political changes are possible.[18] However, there are additional questions about the *local* feasibility of such changes. Some claim that a change from the current system to one based on school designs, charters, vouchers, or contracting would require expenditures that public education budgets cannot support. They note that funds would have to be removed from already strained school budgets to support development of new schools, and that as students left for new schools, existing schools would be forced to eliminate staff and cut programs. These cuts could sharpen concerns about the quality of existing schools and create a strong political backlash.[19]

Proponents of more dramatic reforms claim that the money would be present in public education to pay the necessary transition costs, if only funds were reprogrammed on a per-pupil basis.[20] Financial transitions are possible, they claim, if school district leaders anticipate the changes and move to per-pupil accounting. Such accounting does, however, drastically shift the power in school districts from the central office to schools, which can more readily question the value of central office services. It can also drive wedges among parents, between those who have negotiated special program placements for their children and those who have not.

The difficulties of local politics can be illustrated by the recent history of conflicts within Baltimore's African American community. Under the leadership of a powerful African American legislator, Howard Rawlings, the state of Maryland ordered an overhaul of the Baltimore city schools without regard to any existing rules about job tenure, district structure, or within-district funding practices. The state law also allowed school choice and the possibility of some private school placements for the city's overwhelmingly black school population. Soon after the reform law was enacted, Rawlings was attacked by a coalition of African American group leaders and educators, who accused him of putting the city into the hands of a colonial power. The national NAACP, also led by a prominent Baltimore politician, went on record opposing choice-oriented reform programs, as threats to school integration and black progress. Rawlings retained the strong support of his predominantly African American constituency in the next election, demonstrating the growing appeal to African American parents and voters of dramatic education reforms.[21]

Another aspect of political feasibility relates to the role of labor unions in American public education. Janet Weiss notes that teachers are embedded within an active professional group that transcends boundaries of schools, districts, or even states.[22] The unions play a major role in this professional group, but other components include professional associations and university schools of education, which together shape teacher training, standards for the profession, legislation and regulation, working conditions, and even the status of the profession. All of these associations have, at one time or another, taken decisive stands against what their proponents describe as reform efforts. Herbert Walberg stresses the fact that teachers' unions have actually increased their membership over the past half century, while membership in private sector unions has steadily decreased. With both numbers and dollars behind them, teachers' unions can wield exceptional power on the local, state, and federal levels when issues of school reform are considered.[23]

Questions about political feasibility affect the education reform debate, in ways that the previous chapter's analysis of cause and effect assumptions does not consider. Many people think the inevitable political struggles are worthwhile, especially in light of the desperate problems of school performance that are evident in some big-city schools. Further, as the numbers of parents of all ethnicities who support school choice grows, the "elitism" arguments against such reforms lose much of their force.

Conclusion

This chapter has painted a complex picture of reformers who share strong ideas about what good schools look like and how they are likely to benefit children, but who are so strongly divided by ideology, group loyalties, and economic self-interests that they cannot take one another's ideas seriously. They do not agree on how schools should change or what changes might even be possible.

These divisions are serious, especially in light of the conclusion advanced in chapter 2 that the individual reform proposals are too weak to succeed on their own but could reinforce one another. Rivalries and professional stereotypes are keeping apart people whose ideas might in fact be complementary.

Ideological Hot Buttons 4

THE PRECEDING CHAPTER discussed differences between those who think school improvements can be driven by educators' intrinsic motivations and those who believe that school change must be driven by extrinsic motivators. Reform advocates can differ sharply about how a particular initiative—for example, statewide standards, explicit school designs, or family school choice—would affect important objectives such as school effectiveness and equity of access to good schools.

Table 4-1 summarizes those differences. Are these purely academic disputes, of importance only to people who publish in and read scholarly journals? Or are they important because they constrain and confuse practical discussions about school reform? We think they are important because they can close off options desperately needed by people seeking solutions to the problems of urban public schools.

Disputes about the implications of potential reform initiatives are important because they polarize and overheat discussions that ought to be measured and practical. Issues like the consequences of standards, choice, and competition can become hot buttons that bring out the worst in debaters and intimidate neutral parties. Ideological conflicts that make

Table 4-1. *Predicted Consequences of Reforms Differ by Theory of Motivation*

Reform element	Intrinsic theory	Extrinsic theory
Externally imposed performance standards	Focus effort on what is measured and limit the curriculum	Motivate attention to instruction and student learning
Staff-constructed teaching methods	School unity and commitment	Factionalization and inefficiency
Designs provided by external R&D groups	Uncommitted implementation and staff passivity	Efficient collaboration based on shared premises
Parent involvement through deliberation	Strengthening of school community; parental commitment	Factionalization and domination by a few with intense preferences
Parent choice	Advantages limited to well-informed and intense parents; school forced to put parents' tastes before professional judgment	Formation of school community based on shared beliefs, uniting people of different races and income levels; delegation of family authority to school
Competition among schools	Collaboration destroyed by inter-school rivalries; sweatshop conditions in schools	Disciplined teacher work and school unity; focus on instruction
Management of schools by private parties	Limitation of curriculum to what is measured; cost cutting and profit taking; avoidance of challenging students	Greater flexibility and attention to school productivity; competition and variety; incentives to help diverse students
School-level hiring of teachers	Exploitation of teachers; abandonment of teaching by many who dislike new working conditions; teacher shortages	Improved opportunities and pay for respected teachers; more capable entrants to teaching profession

some issues too hot to handle can put some promising options out of bounds.

Evidence of the heat of these ideological debates can be seen in newsletters published by reform advocates for parents and teachers. Some of these equate standards with thought control, describe the use of schoolwide designs as "coercion of teachers," charge that charter school laws are an attack on the teaching profession, and warn that family choice is a threat to social justice. The most virulent attacks seem reserved for programs that would create differences or competition among schools. One researcher, arguing that religious conservatives favor forms of education "totally incompatible with the constructivist models of learning," concluded that parents who could not accept schools based on modern psychology "should be told to remove their children from the public schools."[1] On choice and competition, as one newsletter published by a federally funded laboratory warned, "remember, markets create inequity."[2]

Our interviews with the originators of major reform proposals produced two striking facts about predictions such as those in table 4-1. First, there is little or no consistent evidence for these predictions, pro or con. Evidence produced is anecdotal, and the anecdotes of the different sides conflict. Second, when pressed, almost all the reform proponents agree that no such predictions can be taken literally, that whether a given initiative produces one result or another depends on the way it is implemented. Thus, for example, whether family choice of schools leads to racial and income separation or to formation of strong communities of interest across income and race lines depends on how choice is implemented. Similarly, whether teacher-developed methods lead to effective or ineffective schools depends on the quality of the ideas and people involved—and on whether teachers have incentives to collaborate or are simply indulging personal preferences.

We hope this chapter will pull the teeth of the hot button issues so that community leaders do not shy away from important reform ideas just because some faction claims they are flawed or dangerous. Though the issues listed above are complex, they are not infinitely so, and they can be mastered with some attention. The intelligent resolution of these issues can open the way to promising education reform options that have been considered too hard or too risky in the past.

Addressing Hot Button Issues

Brookings has begun a national agenda-setting process, involving educators, lay persons, and prominent researchers on key questions such as the following.[3]

The Meaning of School Community

Most people endorse the words "a school should be a community," but many differ on what forms of community are good and how they come about. Some think that good school communities are formed by groups of like-minded people—based on values, interest in subject matter, or acceptance of particular theories of teaching and learning—who come together to provide a defined educational experience for their children. People who favor this form of community emphasize the importance of the school's being an enterprise that attracts families on the basis of specific promises about methods and results.

Others think that school communities formed in this way are dangerous, that they can lead to hostile relations with others who have different preferences.[4] People who fear schools based on affinity also think schools should be communities, but of a different kind. They think a good community is formed by a diverse group of people who develop common ideas through intense deliberation. People who favor this form of community expect schools to model the deliberative process and to involve all parties—parents, neighbors, group representatives, teachers, and administrators—in an ongoing deliberation about the school's methods and performance.

Those who favor an enterprise process think schools are most effective if they are coherent and based on explicit theories of teaching and learning. They believe that control of a school by a small number of people, hiring of staff according to affinity to the school's core strategy, and parental choice all contribute to coherency. They also argue that requiring a school to satisfy the desires of diverse groups of parents and other stakeholders greatly reduces the chance that the school will be coherent, predictable, and effective.

Critics of the enterprise approach to community say that deliberation is much better: instructional methods and curricula chosen through negotiations among diverse interests will not cater to splinter groups. They argue that the shared preferences of small groups are dangerous foundations for public schools, that schools do not need the degrees of coherency desired by those who favor the enterprise process, and that no public school should be exempt from the requirement to respond to diverse needs and demands.[5]

Lorraine McDonnell has encapsulated the dispute in a simple question: To whom do the children belong? Do they belong to the broader society, so that their education should reflect the result of a highly inclusive deliberative process, or do they belong to the parents, so that their education should reflect families' choice of schools that fit family values and aspirations? These questions are not particularly important or hard to resolve in neighborhoods where consensus and trust are strong. But in big cities, where many groups have distinct moral and life-style agendas, and where trust of government institutions is not high, they are extremely difficult to resolve.

Does the fact that opportunities for education are fleeting justify an emphasis on private preferences over public deliberation? Or is acceptance of public decisions about education just another obligation of citizenship?[6] Some claim that public deliberation about schools is like public deliberation about other things: people agree to be bound by the results of political processes, even if they disagree with particular results. Others argue the contrary, that children's education is unlike other issues. In other areas, people accept public decisions they do not like because they know the process is fair and they expect to have a chance to win at some later time. However, a parent who loses in a public debate about how his or her child will be educated (for instance, when a parent who thinks the child needs phonics in a school where other parents and staff are dead set against using it) knows that the loss is permanent: once the child's time in school is past there is no chance to repeat his or her education in a way that the parent would find acceptable. People who do not think they can ever recoup their losses have little incentive to accept a public decision.

Researchers should assume responsibility for finding better-grounded answers to certain questions. What is known about how schools based on the different senses of community operate and how they affect children's learning and their attitudes about tolerance, diversity, and democratic citizenship? In particular, what is the evidence that schools designed for particular groups or intended to convey a distinctive world view lead students to adopt attitudes that threaten social cohesion?[7] In the meantime city leaders should consider these issues unresolved and their importance probably exaggerated by the contending sides. Communities searching for school reform options should not fear trying out approaches that embody different ideas about school community. Aside from conflicting anecdotes, there is no evidence that either of these forms of community is inherently dangerous. Both can lead to good schools, and cities can and should offer both kinds.

Standards

Most education reformers agree that the educational standards movement is a plausible effort to formulate requirements for what students should know and be able to do. Discussing standards can be a very good way to define the public interest in education. However, many educators are skeptical about current government efforts to set standards, in which professional interest groups (e.g., associations of teachers and textbook publishers who specialize in particular subjects) can protect jobs and markets by mandating extensive coverage of particular topics. Some also fear that the sum of many subject-matter standards, each set by people who consider the subject at hand to be supremely important, might burden schools with more requirements than they can meet.

The most enthusiastic proponents of standards think they are both necessary and sufficient to reform schools. The strongest critics are less afraid of standards themselves than of their overzealous use to control everything that is done in schools and to tie student and teacher rewards to microscopically detailed checklists.

In reality, no one has yet created a set of standards that is sufficient unto itself to reform schools, nor a set of standards that can ruin a school that has a clear sense of its mission and has earned the confidence of parents and teachers. The standards discussion will go on for a long time, and it might lead to useful experimentation with how government can balance clarity of goals with school freedom of action. Standards are an important idea, but they can neither reform nor harm schools all by themselves. Local leaders should not be afraid either to set standards or to take other reform actions before standards are fully established.

Meanwhile, researchers will search for answers to questions such as: Are there ways of formulating standards that can guide schools' efforts without driving out diverse approaches to instruction? Are there countervailing pressures (such as a school's need to maintain the confidence of parents and professionals) that can offset the feared effects of external standards? What are the attributes of schools that can respond to official standards of student learning without trivializing what is taught or neglecting important but untested student outcomes?

Teaching Methods

Researchers and journalists have spilled oceans of ink debating whether the best teaching relies on structured presentation of a fixed body of material or teacher-guided exploration, in which student interest determines what is learned at a particular time.

These disputes are heartfelt, and they often turn on harsh words like "regimentation," "indifference about meaning," "making teachers into automatons," "self-indulgent," or "abdication of responsibility."[8] However, these disputes may not reflect consistent differences in real classroom practice. As U.S. secretary of education Richard Riley has noted, skilled teachers use combinations of structured and exploratory methods. Similarly, as the authors' own research has shown, highly coherent schools are extremely clear about what materials students are supposed to learn, but they rely heavily on teacher judgment about how it is to be taught. The distinction between inquiry-based and content-based teaching makes for a good debate, but it probably does not reflect clear differences in school practice.

Modern teaching methods are promising, but they are not the only way children can learn. Local leaders should not let all-or-nothing debates about teaching methods get in the way of practical work on school reform.

Meanwhile researchers will search for answers to questions such as: What are the issues in dispute between those who favor teacher-constructed and exploration-based methods of instruction and those who favor instruction driven by the imperative to teach a specified knowledge base? Does the distinction between inquiry-based and content-based instruction reflect clear differences in school practice, or does most school practice reflect combinations of the two theories? (Are these concepts distinct or do they represent vague and possibly overlapping images of good teaching?) If the two theories can be distinguished empirically, what evidence exists for the distinctive effectiveness of either approach? In the absence of a tradition of rigorous testing of instructional methods (and in the face of one side's belief that best practices cannot be standardized enough to allow such tests), how can this debate be clarified and disciplined by evidence?

Methods of Ensuring Teacher Quality

No one seriously questions the proposition that well-prepared and skillful teachers are more desirable than poorly prepared and less skilled ones. No one seriously argues that it is good for the majority of big-city science and mathematics teachers to lack advanced training in their subjects. But people differ over the best way to ensure the quality of the teaching force. Like the other topics summarized, this one is burdened by unclear assumptions and hidden agendas. Some consider the teaching force as a fixed population of tenured civil servants who have rights to their jobs; the only way to improve teaching is to improve the basic education, motivation, and pedagogical skills of those teachers. Among those who equate improvement of the teaching force with professional development of current teachers, some emphasize starting at the top to create a more enlightened profession while others emphasize improving the knowledge base and skills of the least prepared teachers, especially those in inner cities.

Others think of the teacher supply as elastic, depending on entry requirements, salaries, and working conditions. Teaching can be improved by changing the working conditions in schools so that people of higher ability will want to work in them. Claims that "our teachers can't teach to higher standards unless you [the government or the broader community] retrain them," may be true, but they do not necessarily prove that retraining is the only route to improvement.

Most analysts agree that long-term improvements in teacher performance also require changes in college and university education. Critics fear that massive investments in remedial education for currently employed teachers give colleges and universities, which do not suffer if their graduates are poorly prepared, a free pass. Some claim that the best way to make colleges and universities accountable is to create a competitive market where graduates of weak teacher training programs are at a disadvantage.

No one denies the importance of teachers' continuing to learn and improve throughout their professional lives. But there is strong disagreement about the wisdom and practicality of upgrading a failed urban school system via in-service retraining. Obviously, today's teachers will make up a major share of the teaching force of five and ten years hence. But a teaching force can experience a great deal of turnover in a few years.

Researchers should assume responsibility to find answers to questions like: Can in-service education remedy lack of basic skills and knowledge? Do professional development activities that attract the most intensely interested teachers influence the knowledge and practice of less interested (and possibly less able) teachers? How might different conditions of teacher employment (for example, as offered by charter schools) affect the number and quality of entrants to teaching and the likelihood that the most able graduates of teachers' colleges will stay in teaching? From what populations might new entrants to teaching come? How would the quality of the teaching force be affected by policies that assumed that most teachers would switch back and forth between teaching and other jobs, or that many might enter teaching in mid-career?

However, local leaders need not wait for researchers to do their work. They should not be afraid to invest in ambitious efforts to retrain the weakest teachers, but they should not let teachers escape responsibility for their own performance. Nor should leaders ignore the possibility of creating vacancies and attracting new teachers by increasing the freedom of action of school leaders and teachers.

Competition among Schools

Opinions about the effects of competition on schools are extreme and polarized. Some assume that the average quality of public schools is now about as good as it can get. Competition would create advantages for some schools, and they would get even better. But it would harm other schools, and they would get worse. Others think that the average quality of schools can rise and that competition can make good schools better, can make average schools good, and can lead to replacement of weak schools with better ones.

Many fear that deliberate creation of differences among public schools (all-magnets, charter, or contract schools approaches) would Balkanize student populations. Privileged groups would seek to form exclusive enclaves, and school leaders would compete for easy-to-educate and high-prestige clienteles. Groups with divisive ideologies (particularly right-wing and white and black separatist groups and religious extremists) would find ways to get control of enough schools to serve their clienteles. Working-class families and hard-to-educate groups would be left with school providers who either did not have strong ideologies or could not compete for the more desirable students.

Early studies of charter schools indicate that they admit at least as high a proportion of low-income and minority students as do neighboring public schools.[9] However, many who fear the competition introduced by charter schools say that today's charter schools are under an unusual degree of public scrutiny and that many are run by people dedicated to the equity goals of public education. As the number of charter schools increases, they argue, groups with more exclusive or separatist agendas are likely to gain control of some schools.

There is disagreement both about the numbers of separatist schools that are likely to arise and about the degrees of influence that such schools are likely to have on their students. Some argue that the numbers of parents who would willingly separate their children from the social mainstream are small. The vast majority of parents who now choose private or religious schools do so with the expectation that their children will be well prepared to enter higher education and the economy and to function as citizens. Even those schools that appeal to a highly specialized group of parents intend to prepare their students for full participation in the economy and democratic politics.[10]

We know very little about whether competition would stratify or segregate schools, how many separatist schools would arise, and how they would affect their students. Little objective research has been done on the consequences of students' attending the anti-integrationist white Christian academies; this question is especially poignant in light of the fact that many schools originally founded by whites who wanted to escape school integration now serve African American students.

In general, competition can be an important source of pressure for improvement, and the fact that some educators dread it does not mean that it is not good. However, many schools can improve and maintain quality without competition. Local leaders should not be afraid to include competition as an element of their reform strategies, but they should also feel free to consider broad efforts to improve public schools that do use competition as a motivator for improvement.

Meanwhile, researchers will search for better answers to questions such as: Does competition lead all schools to seek the easiest-to-educate students and shun average or more difficult students? Under what circumstances can competition narrow the curriculum by encouraging schools to focus all their instructional time and energy on the subjects that are tested and publicly reported? Alternatively, does competition encourage schools to specialize, and can it lead to a new supply of schools, including some that are specially adapted to the needs of various disadvantaged groups? What is known about how different forms of competition for students affect school quality and whether all forms of competition inevitably create some schools that are losers? How does competition for students affect school organization, clarity, discipline, consistency, sense of community, and links between school and neighborhood?

Family Choice of Schools

This is the most hotly debated topic on education reform. Some fear that family choice will inevitably lead to a sharp separation between students whose parents care enough about education to make informed

Table 4-2. *Hopeful and Fearful Perspectives on Choice*

Aspect of choice	Hopeful case	Fearful case
Family choice of school	Forces schools to demonstrate performance and keep promises; allows parents to form bonds of trust with school and creates leverage for both parents and schools; permits schools based on value consensus	Puts premium on parental knowledge and initiative; allows advantaged parents to isolate their children from the rest of society; lets weak schools serve undemanding families
School choice of students	Strengthens schools by allowing them to set boundaries on student effort and behavior and make demands of parents; allows schools to construct student bodies that share values but may be diverse in income and race	Allows schools to exclude minority students; creates opportunity for some schools to make exclusiveness part of their appeal; lets weak schools survive by serving the poor; limits deliberation within the school
Teacher choice of schools	Allows teachers to find schools that fit their needs and abilities; forces schools to compete on basis of working conditions and opportunities	Allows ablest teachers to escape the most demanding situations; creates rivalries and limits cooperation; leads to racially segregated faculties
School choice of teachers	Strengthens instructional programs by allowing schools to select teachers on the basis of fit and rewarding high performance; creates opportunities that will attract better people to teaching	Allows exclusion of minority teachers and reduces internal diversity of schools; allows prestige schools to skim the cream, leaving weak teachers to other schools; lets schools exploit teachers, drive down wages; will make teaching unattractive, drive out talent, create shortages

choices and children whose parents do not, and to segregation by race and class. Others regard choice as a fundamental right of families and also an element of strong schools. Chosen schools, they argue, are strengthened by explicit agreements between faculty and family, constructing definite parent expectations and granting the family's authority to the school.[11]

Table 4-2 presents a summary of hopeful and fearful views of choice developed in the course of a Spencer Foundation study of education and democracy.[12]

Critics assert that choice programs create advantages for higher-income, more sophisticated families and promote separation of children by race and class.[13] Anti-choice claims include these: that better-educated families have greater access to information about quality schools; that white middle-class families gain disproportionate access to the most desirable programs, teachers, and schools; that choice programs benefit those children whose families aggressively seek better alternatives and harm those children (mostly minority and low income) whose parents take a more passive approach to education; that schools of choice, including magnets, charters, and privately run institutions, attract the best teachers; that schools that can choose their students seek out the easiest students to educate; that even where supposed lottery admissions procedures are in use, advantaged families find ways of getting their children into those schools with the best reputations; and that even with rigorously fair admissions processes, families with more money and better access to transportation benefit most.

A recent book on choice programs by Harvard professors Gary Orfield, Bruce Fuller, and Richard Elmore makes all these assertions.[14] So does a recent book on privatization by Carol Ascher, Robert Berne, and Norman Fruchter,[15] and a book on magnet schools by Claire Smrekar.[16] Analysts like Smrekar, who understand the advantages of choice as a way to strengthen schools and empower families, are nonetheless worried that it can exacerbate inequalities. Similarly, Terry Moe acknowledges that choice can lead to inequalities and group separation, but argues that well-designed programs can avoid these problems.[17] Recently, many voucher proponents have narrowed their sights to advocate only means-tested vouchers that would benefit only the most severely disadvantaged children.

The chief impediment to a balanced discussion of these potential problems of choice is the absence of a fair standard of comparison. Too often, real data about the sorting effects of choice programs are compared with the current system's pretensions, not its performance. Many criticisms of choice assume that the current public school system is equitable and that the sophisticated and committed cannot manipulate the existing education bureaucracy to create advantages for themselves. Choice proponents counter that the existing system sustains immense inequalities. Highly paid senior teachers can choose where they want to teach, and they cluster in schools in middle-class neighborhoods. This leaves the lowest paid and newest teachers to teach in low-income schools. Consequently, schools in low-income neighborhoods often have less than half the real dollar per pupil expenditures of higher-income schools in the same school district. So-called "desegregated schools" often house minority and white children under the same roof but offer separate and profoundly different instructional programs, based on unequal resource commitments to the two groups.

In general, choice can be a major asset to families, and it can strengthen schools.[18] However, urban reforms that include choice must use random student selection and other methods of ensuring that parents know about and can exercise choices. No such arrangements can completely equalize access and outcomes. Parents have a moral obligation to seek the best learning opportunities for their children, and efforts by parents to gain advantages for their children are endemic to all forms of education, public and private. Under any system of school selection, whether based on choice or on bureaucratic methods now commonly used in big cities, sophisticated families will seek to take advantage of the best opportunities; popular programs can be the most selective; the best teachers will gravitate to schools with the best students and principals; and students with the weakest preparation will often be sorted into less accelerated programs than are stronger students. This is at least as true for the current bureaucratic system as for choice systems.

Researchers are looking for definitive answers to questions like: Do policies that limit the choices of the families still remaining in urban public schools burden the aggressive poor (families that would seek the best available education for their children if they were allowed to choose)?

Are there rules and processes that could minimize the connection between choice and racial or class segregation? Is low-income parents' apparent low level of knowledge and interest in education a fixed attribute, or would the availability of choice lead to greater knowledge, interest, and initiative regarding schooling?

There is no need, however, for local leaders to wait for researchers to come to agreement. People searching for urban school system reform strategies have no need to fear including elements of choice in their reform plans: families can safely choose schools if the district maintains minimum quality standards for all schools and administers a process of random selection among all eligible applicants for a school; schools can safely compete for students if the student selection process is fair; and schools can be free to select the teachers they need if the district enforces normal requirements for teacher qualifications. Once lay leaders initiate reform strategies that include elements of choice, they should also insist that the results be compared against the real performance of the current system, not against some unattained ideal.

The Inevitability of Poor Implementation

A final hot button that stands in the way of almost every promising reform initiative is the fear of incomplete or perverse implementation. Many people oppose particular proposals because they assume that they cannot be well implemented.[19] Though they may have no problem with the theory behind a particular proposal, they do not believe public officials will oversee its implementation well enough to ensure that it does no harm. Table 4-3 summarizes some common fears.

When opposition to a reform idea is based on fears of perverse implementation, criticism is normally stated in the form of a slippery slope argument. The essence of such an argument is that taking a relatively innocuous action sets one on a road that will inevitably lead to a harmful conclusion. Like most forms of argument, slippery slope arguments are sometimes valid and sometimes not. Whether a first step leads inevitably to a disastrous consequence depends on whether there is an obvious principle that can guide the decision about where to stop. Thus the

Table 4-3. *Implementation Risks Raised By Different Proposals*

Reform proposals	Feared implementation problems
Standards	Schools whose students have trouble meeting standards will narrow instruction and emphasize drill-and-practice methods over teaching for understanding
Teacher redevelopment	Enthusiastic teachers will put their own satisfaction and freedom to experiment above interests of students; poorly motivated teachers will not change
School designs	Teachers and principals will put faithful execution of a design above reflection on practice and meeting students' needs; half-implemented designs will worsen the fragmentation of weak schools
Decentralization	Schools will be cut adrift without sources of help and advice; students in bad schools and schools that have parental support despite low performance will suffer
Charters	Groups seeking charters will try to hand-pick students and exclude the poor and minorities; extremists will seek control of charter schools; lax oversight will lead to misuse of public funds
Contracts	Contracts will be let to political favorites and profit-making firms will use a loss-leader strategy to drive community nonprofits out of the market
Vouchers	Public officials will not be able to build strong incentives for creation of schools in minority and low-income areas; schools will be allowed to hand-pick the most desirable students; schools will find ways to charge hidden tuition, thus excluding the poor; and low-income parents will not get the information they need to pick good schools

decision to drink a beer does not put a normal person on a slippery slope toward intoxication and death.

Similarly, setting standards does not in itself cause schools to teach only what will be tested; creating greater freedom for teachers does not inevitably lead to teacher self-indulgence; and allowing private groups to run some public schools does not inevitably lead to discrimination against the poor. Standards need to be balanced with school competition and parental choice. Teacher freedom needs to be constrained by pressure for performance, and school autonomy needs to be limited by publicly enforced rules on fair admissions. As the next chapter will show, no reform plan is self-executing. All must be carefully designed with attention to the causal assumptions they make and the incentives they create. Community leaders must monitor the short-term results of reform initiatives to make sure they are having the effects expected and are not being trivialized or distorted.

Use of the slippery slope argument is a political tactic for people who may wish schools would improve but fear any change in the status quo. The essential job of community leaders, whether elected or appointed, is to make distinctions between beneficial and harmful actions. Courts exist to enforce principles of fairness and political equality. Perverse implementation is not inevitable, and there is no reason to dismiss an educational option just because someone sees it as sloping in some direction.

Conclusion

This chapter has drawn readers through the deepest and most emotional conflicts about public education. Its purpose is not to frighten but to demythologize. These conflicts are serious, but many of them are more ideological and theoretical than real. There is no reason why local leaders searching for ideas about reform should shy away from family choice, school competition, or novel ideas about improving the teaching force. Similarly, leaders do not have to search for the one best instructional method or set of standards to guide instruction. These ideals do not exist, and the best approach is to try many plausible approaches rather than to place all bets on one.

Researchers like the authors of this report have a responsibility to shed the light of real evidence on those issues that have become ideological hot buttons. Local leaders should not let such academic conflicts distract them from the practical trial-and-error business of school reform. Knowing that the most fervent conflicts are not based on facts should help lay leaders keep ideologically motivated assertions in perspective.

Creating Reforms That Can Work 5

I N MANY big cities, noneducators are being asked to create rescue strategies for the public schools. In Cleveland and Chicago, mayors have taken control of the school system and are searching for ways to transform failed schools and raise student achievement across the board. In the District of Columbia, as in Baltimore, lay reform boards have been asked both to navigate a school system through its day-to-day crises and to create a new strategy that will substantially increase performance.

These assignments to noneducators arise out of desperation. In these cities and many more, successive school boards and superintendents have been unable to unite educators on an improvement strategy. In part the problems of uniting for action are political, as discussed above. But some of the barriers to united action are intellectual. People do not know how to start, and much of the available expert advice comes in the form of a sales pitch (buy my silver-bullet teaching materials or my new teacher-training program, and it will set off changes that will make all children succeed) or a double-bind admonition (you must rescue the children, but you must avoid any changes in teachers' and administrators' assignments or working conditions).

Today's mayors, civic and foundation leaders, and school boards must therefore construct new solutions. Like new management teams taking over troubled businesses, they need to avoid being drawn into every issue that concerns people inside the system. They need to devise change strategies that are sophisticated enough to improve the performance of a very complex organization, yet are simple enough to integrate the efforts of many people. Distilling what has been learned from our own study—including case studies of local reform efforts and city reform simulation exercises,[1] plus others' studies of partially successful efforts to reform big-city school systems[2]—we offer suggestions to help those newly responsible for reforming city school systems.

How to Get Started

City leaders faced with a new responsibility can easily feel flooded with demands and unable to find a place to start. However, there are ways to make the problems manageable.

Separate Immediate Management from Long-Term Planning

The cycle of urban school reform is characterized by long periods of stagnation punctuated by terrible emergencies. This is particularly true when school system problems become so severe that the mayor or the state government is forced to disband the school board and create a whole new management structure, as has recently happened in Cleveland, Chicago, Washington, D.C., Baltimore, and Trenton and Paterson, New Jersey, and is sure to happen elsewhere.

The emergency can become especially severe if a group of community leaders is forced both to deal with the school system's daily crises and to create a reform that can make a difference in the long run. In such situations, short-term disasters readily drive out long-term thinking. The lay board in Baltimore, for example, was forced to divide into a number of committees with executive powers. Board members spent so much time on immediate issues such as personnel, bus routes, building maintenance, and complaints about misuse of funds that they had little opportunity to talk together, take advice, or formulate long-term options for discussion. The District of Columbia lay board faced similarly grave emergencies (in particular a court order that prevented schools from opening in 1997 until all roof, furnace, and plumbing repairs were complete). These issues fell even more strongly on them when the specially appointed chief executive, retired U.S. Army general Julius Becton, resigned under fire about financial and property management. The Chicago reform board was able to rely on a strong chief executive operating under the mayor's personal authority. Of all the emergency boards appointed to rescue city school systems, only Chicago's was able to concentrate on long-term issues.

In general, short-term crises drive out long-term thinking. City school districts are generally in desperate straits financially, managerially, and educationally. Questions of student safety, labor unrest, and charges of criminal misuse of public funds grab attention, and work on creating a new school system that could educate children more effectively can get neglected. Unions often demand assurances that no workers will be reassigned and no jobs will be lost before leaders can fully understand the consequences of such commitments. School boards and civic leaders should segment their work to ensure that at least some members are free to work on the district's long-term school performance problems. An executive committee should handle day-to-day matters without making long-term commitments, so other members can think ahead, as discussed below.

Even as school board members and civic leaders focus on specifically educational issues, they should separate short- and long-term issues. Educationally, the short-term issue is almost always one of student reading proficiency. Elementary-level students, especially low-income minority children, fall rapidly behind national averages, and shockingly low numbers of secondary school students are competent readers.

School boards and civic leaders can address students' direst reading problems even as they are considering more fundamental structural reforms in the public education system. As participants in the decision-making simulations used by the Brookings study have suggested, reading scores can be raised on an emergency basis by creating special triage programs for children whose reading scores are near enough to meeting state standards so that a period of accelerated work might put them over the top. This triage arrangement would temporarily assign every certified teacher who was not assigned to regular classroom duty (including the many certified teachers who normally work in the central office) to teach reading in schools where large numbers of students had scores only slightly below state reading standards. This is certainly not a long-term solution, but it could lead to prompt increases in the numbers of students who meet state standards and establish the principle that focused effort improves performance.

Alternatively, a district could temporarily mandate that every student and every teacher in every school spend half of every school day on reading instruction. Drafting every teacher in the district for this purpose would allow schools to create small homogeneous classes for intense instruction.

Such expedients are not permanent reforms, but they could make a big enough dent in performance deficits to forestall state takeovers or collapses in public confidence. They could also set the stage for broader and more lasting reforms by showing that strikingly different uses of person-power and instructional time are possible and can produce results.

Look for the Roots of the Problem

When a school system fails students and continues failing despite changes of leadership and many successive reform efforts, there is no escaping the conclusion that the problem is built into the system itself. There is always a temptation to settle for a quick-acting, single-factor solution—for example, a new after-school tutoring program, enough new teachers to lower class size by a few percentage points, new attitude adjustment sessions for teachers—that can avoid the pain of a thorough rethinking of the way the school system does business. However, when a city school system's performance has fallen to the point where it is threatened by state or judicial takeover, or where parents who can escape the schools are doing so, showy short-term solutions are not enough. Board members have to start asking how they can reengineer the school system so that failure is not endemic.

City public school systems are now government agencies run by civil servants and operating under rules made by political decisionmaking bodies. School boards make policies in response to political pressures. Even when the pressures abate, the rules remain, teaching staffs are held in place by collective bargaining agreements, and staff members in the central office supervise schools from specialized perspectives (such as compliance with federal program requirements and observance of the provisions in teacher contracts). The result is that every school becomes host to many programs and requirements, each focused on a particular problem or beneficiary. These separate efforts compete for the time and attention of teachers, administrators, and students, and they often end up getting in one another's way.

The current system is built to make schools responsive to mandates and political bargains, past and present, made by the state legislature or the local school boards. And the system works: schools attend to these matters. Teachers and principals accept the constraints imposed by such mandates and try to work within them. However, compliance does not equal effectiveness. Schools that are dominated by mandates and compliance issues are seldom as attentive to quality of instruction and student learning as they need to be. Effective schools—especially those most successful with disadvantaged students—are not preoccupied with rules or adult job protections. They are united by a vision of what students need to learn and how adults must work together on instruction.

If the work of a reform board is to have lasting results, the board must start at the beginning, asking what kinds of schools we want for our children, what prevents our having them now, and how we can build a system that will support, not prevent, such schools. Subsequent sections suggest how that can be done.

Where to Get Help

Local leaders do not need to go it alone. They can ask for help from sources that will not try to co-opt or dominate their decisions.

Rely on an Outside Institution as a Critical Friend

School boards and groups of civic leaders ultimately need to make their own plans and solve their local problems, but they can be greatly strengthened by an outside critical friend. An outside organization that can work with the local board in confidence, answering questions, gathering data, and reflecting on the experience of other cities, can be indispensable.

Such a critical friend can follow events in the city but can stand above the local fray and refocus or introduce important ideas that have gotten lost. It can also help remind local leaders that short-term crises must not blur their focus on long-term strategy making and restructuring and can help create local capacity to monitor successes and failures.[3] There are sources of such help. Some localities have joined national networks with others struggling to reform. The National Alliance for Restructuring, part of the National Center for Education and the Economy in Washington, D.C., provides this form of help for communities that want to use standards as the driver of reform. The New American Schools (NAS) Corporation also provides consultants and advisors for school districts interested in adopting NAS-sponsored new school designs. RAND has provided broad assistance to community-wide strategic planning in Pittsburgh and Cleveland. The Education Commission of the States (ECS), an interstate compact dedicated to disseminating promising practices nationwide, has provided this form of assistance in a number of localities. In the future, Brookings will use the lessons from this project in teaming with ECS to provide critical friend assistance.

All these organizations require at least partial payment for their services, and the best funding sources are local foundations and businesses. Few struggling school systems have the available money for these purposes; private funding also ensures that the critical friend organization will not be crippled by political constraints.

Assemble Diverse Groups of Experts to Get beyond Local Politics

School board members and other local leaders put in charge of school reform face a welter of pressures and demands. Vendors urge investments in instructional technology. Central office staff members and university professors propose adoption of new curricula and grade-level reorganization. Taxpayer groups demand better fiscal accounting and improved personnel systems. Teachers' unions and other employee groups seek assurance that no jobs will be lost. Parents who have worked out special placements for their children demand that "good programs" be left alone. "Friends of public education" groups urge pressure on the state for more money as a prerequisite for change.

Many of these ideas may be good and necessary. But school boards and civic leadership groups that try to accommodate all these demands quickly find themselves doing a little of everything without a definite strategy for turning the school system around. There is a difference between a strategy—a set of coordinated actions designed to complement one another in resolving a complex problem—and a series of unrelated actions taken one by one in response to the pressures of the moment. Local leaders who follow the series-of-unrelated-actions approach will recreate the problems they were appointed to correct. Though public education is often condemned for its resistance to change, it does not reject new ideas. On the contrary, big-city school systems often encompass almost every imaginable approach to instruction and reform. Many good ideas often operate at small scale, usually in isolation and sometimes in competition with one another.

Local leaders need expert help getting beyond abstract options so they can move toward devising sets of complementary actions with clear implementation plans, assignments of administrative responsibility, funding schemes, performance indicators and timetables, and midcourse assessment plans.

School reform experts—the very people whose differences of opinion and feuds have been described in earlier chapters—are indispensable sources of ideas and strategies. However, local school boards and groups of civic leaders should not deal with such experts one by one. They should consult with experts in groups, using their critical friend organization to challenge experts who advance specific points of view to acknowledge the limitations of their own ideas and craft plans that incorporate the strengths of competing ideas.[4]

One important function of a critical friend organization is to assemble a group of education reform experts who represent competing schools of thought. As we have found in the course of the Brookings study's simulation exercises, expert groups that include economists, political scientists, and people knowledgeable about private education, as well as educators and experts in testing and teacher professional development, provide much broader and more logically complete reform advice than do more narrowly composed groups.

There are many advantages of dealing with such experts in teams, not the least of which is that debate (and the critical friend organization) can keep individuals honest and prevent local leaders from being swayed in different directions as individual experts barnstorm through town.

Businesses and foundations also need to make sure they do not fractionate local leaders' strategies by offering funding for one-sided or magic-bullet solutions. Funders are as susceptible as anyone else to being seized by enthusiasm for plausible but incomplete initiatives; they need to support the effort to create a balanced and logically complete strategy. This can be accomplished if local private funders pay the expenses of the critical friend organization and the diverse panel of experts discussed above and pledge to support the whole reform strategy that emerges.

Relying on carefully balanced groups of experts also helps construct definite options that can become the object of local public discussion. Plans assembled by experts are likely to be bolder and better organized than reform plans that bubble up from unstructured local political processes. They are also more likely than politically generated plans to withstand criticism. Skilled leaders can force people with objections to explain how the plan can be changed without destroying its overall effectiveness.

Seek Help from the State

By the time local elected and community leaders have been placed in charge of a city school system, it is likely that the state department of education will have tried everything it can think of to help the city. That does not mean, however, that state officials cannot help. They can relieve a city of many burdensome rules that would otherwise strictly limit local reform strategies. State officials also have strong incentives to help, since big cities that have been taken over by lay leaders are often seen as major liabilities for the whole state.

City school systems receive funds from many state sources and from federal programs managed by the state department of education. Such programs often have stringent rules about how funds can be used. Reformers often find that city school systems have a great deal of money but are forced to spend it inefficiently.[5] City school systems are often unable to convert funds earmarked for transportation to other uses, such as teacher hiring. They often have a substantial amount of money for teacher training, but it is divided into so many small tightly controlled accounts that no comprehensive teacher training strategy is possible. Federal and state funds for remedial education of disadvantaged students are also held in separate accounts and dedicated to specific teachers and the services they provide. Taken together, program regulations and spending controls can create gridlock.

State governments are, however, able to make remarkably flexible arrangements for leaders of troubled school systems who can say what they need and why. State leaders in Ohio, for example, have found ways to grant almost any waiver requested by reform leaders in Cleveland and Cincinnati. Many states can also make greater use of flexibility provisions of the recently amended elementary and secondary education act (ESEA). The largest ESEA program, Title 1, now allows almost any low-income inner-city school to use its funds for schoolwide improvement efforts.

Some federal regulations are harder to waive, especially those connected with civil rights and services to the disabled. However, local administrators' interpretations of those rules are often more restrictive than necessary. Chicago found, for example, that the U.S. Justice Department had a far more flexible view of how charter schools could serve disabled children than did the city's own civil rights unit.

In general, local leaders should not accept the first thing they hear about what is permissible and what cannot be done. They should seek advice and cooperation from high-level state and federal officials, including their governor and the U.S. secretary of education.

How to Construct a Reform Package Bold Enough to Work

Problems as deeply ingrained as those of urban public education cannot be solved by timid measures. There are ways that local leaders can avoid having their options constrained by the preferences and interests of people within the system.

Avoid a Stakeholder Strategy

Community leaders are inevitably tempted to assemble the heads of organizations that run public education—the teacher's union, principals, central office personnel, custodians, and the PTA—to hammer out a new reform strategy. This approach has the advantage of showing respect for the people who work in public education day to day. It has the disadvantage of returning the initiative to the very people who have found ways of living comfortably with the status quo. Stakeholder groups have accommodated themselves to the barriers that prevent school improvement. Some have members who believe any change will hurt them. Even parent groups can be captured by families that have gained the best public school placements for their children. Most of them sincerely want schools to improve, but they know and believe all the reasons why no serious initiative is feasible.

Community leaders need to be realistic about the jobs and career commitments of superintendents, central office administrators, teachers' union heads, and principals. With the rare exception of a superintendent recruited from businesss or the military, all have made careers within the existing public education structure and have reason to be loyal to people like themselves. Some leading individuals from these groups—including, in many cities, the leader of the teachers' union—may see the need for the change and even be able to take personal risks to promote it. But the need to protect the jobs, incomes, satisfaction, and benefits of their constituents inevitably limits the changes that union leaders and other stakeholder representatives can propose or openly support.[6]

Stakeholders have legitimate roles, but they should be consulted after community leaders have made their own assessment of the situation and identified, usually with outside help, some potential reform strategies. Reform leaders must also manage their relationships with stakeholders to maximize freedom of action. In their own professional roles, many civic leaders run churches, companies, foundations, charitable institutions, and colleges and universities. They know how to listen to the stakeholders in the organizations they lead without giving anyone a veto over a necessary line of action. Leaders need to use these same skills in their efforts to reform public education. As in every other field, leadership takes time and attention, and it involves more than finding the golden mean among all organized groups.

Redesign the System around Strong Schools

Effective schools are alike in some ways and different in others. All are simple, focused on student learning, collaborative, personalized, responsive, willing to face and overcome their own weaknesses, and open to parents. Effective schools differ in the instructional methods and materials they choose, how they select and train their teachers, and how they help students who are struggling to learn.

Unfortunately, leaders responsible for education reform often confuse the aspects of effective schools that should vary from school to school with those that should be the same. Thus school boards and other civic leadership groups often struggle with questions like what texts and instructional methods all schools should choose, how all teachers should be retrained, and by what formal processes struggling students should get help.

A reform plan must start with the commitment to create a system of public governance and oversight that fosters strong, distinctive schools. Unfortunately, if these issues are settled by citywide deliberation and mandated for all schools, maintaining necessary differences among schools becomes impossible. Teachers and principals cannot make the choices necessary to take advantage of the specific strengths of their students and teachers. Lack of freedom drives out initiative and responsibility and fosters concern for compliance—thus recreating the weaknesses of the education system that reform was supposed to remedy.

Leaders responsible for creating a reform strategy need to make sure schools have the freedom and opportunity to develop integrative capital, as defined in chapter 2. Coherent, productive schools arise from the interaction of ideas about instruction and from hard, collaborative work among teachers. The adults in a school must work together to decide many things: how to put basic ideas into practice; how to judge whether students are progressing satisfactorily; how to adapt the instructional program when students are not learning all they should or when society demands that students learn new things; when to collaborate and when to work independently; when to compromise and when to allow dissidents to split off. The authors' new research on schools high in integrative capital demonstrates:

—The centrality of ideas. Coherent schools are not slavishly devoted to cloning other schools, but all use some existing conception of how a school might operate as a starting point for their own development. Some are based on the writings of theorists like Montessori or consciously imitate successful schools. Some rely on frequent contact with living educational theorists or organizations, like Robert Slavin's Success for All or the New American Schools design teams.

—The importance of collaboration. Coherent, productive schools leave nothing to chance. School leaders understand the importance of teacher collaboration and problem solving, and they engage teachers in decisions that matter to them. Leaders also directly manage staff hiring and socialization as processes that can profoundly affect school climate and performance.

—Neither ideas nor process is sufficient. Unless guided by ideas about instruction, no process is likely to create a coherent, productive school. Schools that try to increase productivity via group process without strong guiding principles have been unable to create the degree of staff cooperation required for productive work. Similarly, good ideas without a strategy for implementation change nothing.

Several steps are essential in developing a school high in integrative capital:

—Start with one or a few individuals with ideas about how a school can work and what students should know. This can be done by offering outstanding local teachers and principals the opportunity to describe the kind of school they would create, by issuing a request for proposals that allows anyone with an idea to propose a school plan (this has been done with some success in Chicago and in Dade County, Florida), or by hiring an organization that is in business to run schools, including some of the New American Schools design teams and for-profit firms like Advantage, Edison, Sabis, and Alternative Public Schools.

— Make the ideas behind each individual school as explicit and pub-lic as possible so that teachers and parents who consider the school can understand what is offered and expected.

—Expect that schools will be different from one another, both be-cause groups of children are not all alike and because there are many approaches to education that can work as long as they are put into prac-tice by people who believe in them and have the freedom to implement the approach rigorously.

—Support the development of a tradition of strong and authoritative leadership in the new schools by supporting action consistent with the school plan and avoiding mandates that compromise or divert resources from the school plan.

—Encourage individual schools to build strong external constituen-cies of three kinds: customers (families who trust the school and rely on it to educate their children); external supporters (donors and intellec-tual mentors who buttress the school financially and educationally); and validators (employers and higher-level schools to which students aspire and that can provide feedback on the school's performance).

—Ensure that school leaders have control of funds and key decisions about hiring and curriculum and encourage leaders in individual schools to take the initiative with parents and the public, asserting what the school hopes to attain, where it is now failing, and what it will do next.

None of these steps is easy. Starting a school from scratch is difficult, but turning around a school with a tradition of low expectations and lax work habits is even harder. Reflecting these difficulties, most private and independent schools start with a model or exemplar in mind—an edu-cational philosopher whose ideas they intend to put into practice or a school elsewhere that they hope to imitate. They do not require staff to invent everything for themselves or to meld warring factions into a co-herent organization. Many coherent schools are started by people who have worked in exemplar schools and want either to provide a similar school to a new community or to improve on what they regard as an essentially sound model. Some are formed by groups hived off from ex-isting schools; founders self-consciously build their school around a core staff of people who share commitments and past experiences.

Imitating successful schools is surely an underused method for creating strong schools and transforming weak ones. But there is also a place for new designs that show how a school's pedagogy, staffing, student life, and client relationships can be integrated. There is also a place for people and organizations who can help many schools develop the forms of integrative capital that school leaders, staff, or communities choose. The New American Schools Corporation has supported a few exemplary designs,[7] but their design teams are able to support only a few schools.[8] Congress has recently enacted the Porter-Obey bill, which will support creation and validation of some additional designs.

Restructure Schools' Incentives, Capabilities, and Opportunities

No one can say in the abstract exactly what overall reform strategy a locality should create for itself or guarantee that any one combination of initiatives will work in all settings. But we can say that every systemwide reform strategy must create incentives for school performance, ways of increasing school capabilities, and opportunities and freedom for school staff members to change the ways they serve students.[9]

These three elements of the reform of a whole big-city system work together. The incentives side of reform is the most familiar and the most obvious. For ten years, school improvement efforts have recognized that performance pressures in public education are too weak. In some areas, schools can fail students for generations without being closed or fundamentally changed. It is also possible for teachers and principals, protected by civil service status, to continue working for a long time without doing a good job. Reform is not supposed to expose teachers and schools to unnecessary or unsympathetic criticism, but it must make it clear that performance matters. It does so simply by emphasizing children's learning, rewarding schools and individuals that make a positive difference, and removing children from situations where they are not learning. No reform is possible if adults are secure in their jobs whether or not they or their schools perform for children.

A reform strategy must increase school capabilities by investing in new ideas, new methods of instruction, teacher training, and recruitment of new teachers if current ones cannot improve. Schools might improve to some degree on their own, but the dramatic increases needed in student learning require expertise that many struggling inner-city schools now lack. Schools need help devising improvement plans and assessing their own progress. Many current teachers need to refresh their subject matter knowledge, and some need to upgrade their basic skills. Schools need to be able to fill teacher vacancies with the best available people, not just those who are on the top of the civil service transfer list. New methods, books, computerized databases, advice, and training will not all appear spontaneously. They will have to be created by state, local, and private investment, and they will have to be made available to schools that have the incentives to use them.

The opportunity dimension of a reform strategy is equally important but less well recognized. School-level initiative is the engine of reform. The changes that matter will happen at the school level, and the only test of a reform is whether it leads to better instruction and increased student learning. Too often, however, teachers and principals feel that they are caught in a web of rules, job protections, and spending constraints that does not allow them to innovate, experiment, or quickly abandon an initiative that is not producing results. Schools need opportunities. They need to be relieved of rules that limit and routinize instruction, and they need to be free to use staff and money in creative ways. Some think schools will ultimately need more money, and they might. But the first thing they need is the opportunity to make full use of the money and talents they now have.

Use the Different Reform Theories as Building Blocks

Civic leadership groups and school boards do not have to invent reform strategies from scratch. The different theories of reform discussed above are excellent building blocks for a broad city school improvement strategy.

Table 5-1 summarizes the strengths and weaknesses of the different philosophies, how well they provide incentives, capabilities, and opportunity. Clearly, no one philosophy is strong in all ways, and a school board or other community leadership group that tried to pursue one to the

Table 5-1. *No One Philosophy Does Everything Necessary to Encourage a System of Strong Schools*

	School performance incentives	Increasing school capabilities	Opportunity for schools to improve
Teacher development	Weak: depends on individual motivation	Strong: focuses on teacher knowledge and skills	Weak: does not increase time for teacher learning or freedom of action
Standards	Weak: establishes goals, not consequences	Moderate: focuses attention on school performance weaknesses	Weak: does not increase time for improvement or freedom of action
School Designs	Weak: design use depends on individual motivation, group consensus	Strong: designs promote schoolwide strategy for child and adult learning	Moderate: designs guide efficient use of time, money
Decentralization	Mixed: seldom clarifies expectations and consequences for school performance	Moderate: seldom gives schools control of money to invest in training, materials	Moderate: exhorts schools to take initiative but does not establish freedom of action
Charters	Mixed: creates strong performance incentives for charter holders, not for others	Moderate: charter defines school mission and approach but does not give detailed guidance	Mixed: creates great freedom of action for charter holders, not for others
Contracts	Strong: creates powerful performance incentives for all schools	Moderate: contract defines school mission and approach but does not give detailed guidance	Strong: creates great freedom of action for all schools
Vouchers	Strong: creates powerful performance incentives for all schools	Weak: does not guide school improvement efforts	Strong: creates great freedom of action for all schools

exclusion of all others would probably fail to produce the degree of school improvement it sought.

A citywide reform strategy designed to capitalize on the complementary strengths of the different reform strategies could be more effective than any big-city reform that has been tried to date. Leaders should consider ways of mixing and matching reform philosophies—not in the spirit of allowing everyone in the school district to do his or her own thing, but in an effort to create a coordinated districtwide reform strategy. Table 5-2 suggests several coordinated strategies that emphasize the strengths of the different philosophies. Leaders should consider these and other mixed strategies that combine a philosophy that creates strong performance incentives with one or more others that provide school-level flexibility and efforts to increase school capabilities.

All combined strategies are not equal. In table 5-2, strategy 1 is probably easiest to implement because it most closely resembles the current system. However, it requires degrees of school control of dollars and staff selection that no public school system now allows.[10] Its reliance on centrally selected curricula and materials also limits schools' freedom of action and accountability for results. Strategy 2 creates performance incentives, but it also relies on centrally controlled assistance to schools. It too leaves the regulatory structure of public education intact, relying on waivers (which many teachers and principals have come to distrust as ambiguous and unreliable) to create opportunities for school change. Strategy 3 is a thorough departure from current practice, combining fundamental deregulation, diverse school providers, performance accountability, parental choice, and multiple sources of assistance to schools.[11]

These are not the only ways of creating combined reform strategies, and leaders in every community will face their own combinations of needs, political constraints, and opportunities. But any possible combined strategy should be assessed on the basis of how well it promotes school incentives, opportunities, and capabilities.

Get beyond the Politics of Hope

In many of our largest and most troubled cities (New York, Los Angeles, Cleveland, Washington, D.C.), every one of the reform ideas we have

Table 5-2. *Some Possible Combined Strategies and How They Provide Incentives, Capabilities, and Opportunities*

Strategies	Incentives	Capabilities	Opportunities
Strategy 1: Decentralization within the system, using standards, contracting and whole-school designs	School-specific performance agreements with superintendent or school board, specifying which schoolwide design the school will follow and how it will meet state standards; expectation that schools will follow distinctive approaches to instruction	District investment in new curriculum, materials, and technology; creation of new teacher training system responsive to individual school needs	School control over high proportion of funds, school hiring of staff, school specification of staff development needs
Strategy 2: A highly centralized system, using standards and major teacher development investments	Close performance-based supervision of school principals by superintendent; expectation that all schools use district-sanctioned standard methods and be assessed via state standards	District investment in new curriculum, materials, and technology; central office provides extensive teacher training opportunities	Schools free to request specific waivers to allow tailoring of standard methods to student needs

| Strategy 3: A system with diverse providers, using whole-school designs, charters, contracting, standards, and vouchers | Every public school has a distinctive contract or charter that specifies the school's design or approach to instruction; parents can choose schools; new schools can be chartered to replace failing schools; and lowest-achieving students can get vouchers to attend private schools | District promotes formation of many independent non-profit providers of curricular advice, instructional materials, and teacher training; schools purchase their own advisers and providers of assistance | Schools control all funds, hire staff, and purchase assistance; are accountable only to provide services promised and show students' results; a central office has only two functions: supporting the board in making agreements with individual schools and assessing school performance in terms set by these agreements |

discussed is operating in some form—present in some schools but not others or engaging some teachers within a single school while others pursue a contrary course. Because they operate separately, the potential complementarities of different reform initiatives are lost and their conflicts are maximized.

Cause-and-effect thinking—drawing all the links between a proposed initiative and the ultimate goal of improving student learning—can eliminate muddle and overcome destructive rivalries. It does so by establishing a higher standard for reform proposals, as explained in chapter 2. The current, lower standard is plausibility: is there some logical connection between a reform proposal (for example, investment in a new curriculum or testing system) and student achievement? The plausibility standard does not require proponents to identify the proposal's limitations or the ways in which other factors might nullify its effects.

Local civic leaders need to insist that reforms be thought through as carefully as business plans. People who run large organizations and businesses must not, as some educators observe, check their brains at the door when they get involved with public schools. Civic leaders must also discipline school superintendents and other government officials, who can otherwise survive by playing the politics of hope, or who can build support for themselves by professing that all children can learn, yet do nothing to make it happen. The core of the politics of hope is the constant creation of glittering new proposals, each of which generates excitement and sympathy for a period of months or years, until it is demonstrably not having any effect, at which time a new proposal is required. School superintendents who operate this way accomplish less, but sometimes keep their jobs longer, than those who pursue definite and consistent reform strategies.

How to Make Sure Plans Will Make a Difference

No strategy can be perfect the first time. Local leaders need to try promising approaches, observe the results, and make adjustments.

Pursue Multiple Approaches

The results of the community simulations used by the Brookings study team demonstrate that local leaders need not search for just one districtwide solution. No one knows enough at any one time to prescribe a solution that will work for all schools or for an indefinite period. As earlier reform efforts have demonstrated, reform initiatives that transform some schools might leave others untouched. Chicago, for example, in 1989 decentralized control over school funds to elected local site councils. This reform led to dramatic changes in approximately one-third of elementary schools but did not touch any high school.[12] Subsequently, Chicago diversified its reform effort to create entirely different sets of incentives and capabilities increases for high schools and to deal differently with schools that improved under local site council control and those that did not. Chicago also created a strong citywide school performance accountability system and vested the power to close and replace failed schools in its superintendent.

Some of the most imaginative reform strategies include trying several promising approaches in different parts of a district, monitoring their results, and either expanding successful experiments and abandoning those that do not work, or combining key elements of different initiatives into new plans that can be tested on a modest scale. The Brookings study's simulations have revealed promising examples of this experimental approach: a small-schools plan that breaks up one-third of the district's elementary schools into small schools, each occupying a part of an existing school building; massive retraining in schools where climate is positive and effort is high but instruction is not improving; use of charters to create competition for low-performing or stagnant schools, especially middle and high schools; and district-managed closure and reconstitution of failed high schools. Careful monitoring of the results of such coordinated initiatives could lead to an evolving but always coherent reform strategy.

Terminate Unsuitable Arrangements

Members of school boards and civic leadership groups need to decide what the school system will no longer do as well as what it will do in the future. In particular, a reform strategy that relies on school-level initiative and that tries to maximize schools' choices of assistance options cannot simultaneously support a school central office that uses all the available school assistance funds to pay civil service salaries. Leaders who intend schools to make their own budgetary decisions cannot simultaneously support a central audit function that requires schools to justify every deviation from a standardized expenditure plan.

There is no way to sugarcoat the fact that the existing system is buttressed—and potential reforms are hampered—by central office structures and collective bargaining agreements whose weaknesses led to the current crisis.

Experts differ on exactly what form the central office should take. But there is broad agreement on an alternative vision—that the central office should exist for the sole purpose of performing irreducibly public functions, such as authorizing schools to receive public funds, assessing the productivity of individual schools and the district as a whole, ensuring that there is a large enough supply of effective schools to permit every student to attend one, and helping students to find better alternatives if the schools have failed them. Schools would still need assistance, technical advice, staff training, and business-oriented services such as accounting, building maintenance, insurance, and legal representation. Some of these might still be offered by school district central offices, but schools cannot enjoy flexibility and be responsible for their own productivity if they cannot choose where they get help. Whenever possible, schools should be able to choose among independent service providers. Central offices should not be able to tax schools, and their income for services provided the schools should come from voluntary fees. Many extra-school functions would ultimately be provided by networks formed by the schools themselves, organizations funded by businesses and foundations, and private fee-for-service vendors.

Central offices would not employ large numbers of staff development, curriculum, or compliance specialists. The central administration could provide basic accounting and funds-allocation services for schools, and it would maintain a small staff to help schools find sources of assistance. The central office could also offer some services, such as building maintenance, food service, payroll, and negotiation with insurance and annuity providers, on a fee basis and at the discretion of individual schools. Central offices might staff or sponsor parent information centers.

Without the responsibility for instructional coordination and school operations, central administrative offices should need fewer employees.

To ensure that future superintendents are not hamstrung by past staff choices, most central office employees would serve at the pleasure of the superintendent, not as tenured civil servants. The money saved by trimming district administration would go directly to the schools.

Lay Out Timelines and Measures of Progress

Too often, local reform initiatives are set in motion without any specific plans for overseeing their operation or measuring their effects. No one can tell the difference between an effective reform or a dead one until many years later. City leaders should follow the example of Chicago, where a University of Chicago–based Consortium for School Reform has conducted hard-nosed assessments of whether schools have changed as expected. A mixture of good and bad news has forced city leaders and educators to strengthen an initially incomplete reform. The result is that Chicago leaders have not enjoyed many periods of blissful confidence that their initiatives will magically transform the schools. However, Chicago now probably has the best thought-through education reform strategy of any big city.

Chicago's monitoring strategy was devised by an independent, university-based organization. Though the school system has provided logistical support, the lion's share of funds for the monitoring program has come from local foundations and business. The multi-university Consortium on Chicago School Research is responsible for data analysis. The consortium asks others' advice on its publications, but it is free to publish results, calling the facts as the consortium sees them.

School boards and civic leaders need to insist that strategies be thought through as carefully as business plans. Establishing standards, performance baselines, benchmarks against which to measure progress, and a rigorous monitoring capability are all essential elements of a reform strategy. Monitoring plans are also good checks of the logic of a reform: if it is impossible to say what a reform effort should be accomplishing at some future time, it is very unlikely that the strategy can be effective.

Lay leaders are understandably eager to return control of the school system to professionals and elected board members. However, they must not abdicate responsibility before they establish a clear strategy of reform against which professionals can be held accountable as well as principles of progress assessment, continuous improvement, and cause-and-effect thinking.

Conclusion

Any city's reform effort can take a decade. That is a tragically long time, given the costs to children. However, unless education reform is taken seriously, as an effort requiring serious thinking, testing, careful use of evidence, and continuous refinement, America's urban public schools are likely to be no better off in ten years than they are now.

Cities can create reform strategies that make a difference. But many things must change. Scholars who invent and advocate reform ideas must adopt principles of truth-in-advocacy and swear off old habits of parallel play (working independently as if their efforts were not interdependent). Funders—national foundations that support reform initiatives and local businesses and foundations that support local reforms—must adopt the discipline of cause-and-effect thinking and refuse to be captured by ideas that are too one-sided to work. Education professionals, including teachers and their union leaders, must accept adult responsibility and make jobs contingent on performance.[13] Finally, local authorities, including mayors, school boards, superintendents, and civic leaders, must resist adopting feel-good and quick-fix reforms and commit to hard-nosed evaluation and continuous strengthening of reform initiatives.

Brookings Program Plans | 6

CITY LEADERS searching for strategies to transform failed school systems now have access only to fragmentary proposals from competing reform entrepreneurs. To bring all the available ideas fully to bear on the problems of urban education, the chasms among competing schools of thought must be bridged. Collaboration among leaders of different reform movements requires new incentives and opportunities for cooperative work.

A new Brookings program will provide an institutional home for the necessary collaboration. It will involve reform innovators, evaluators, policymakers, and local community leaders in an ongoing effort to strengthen the repertoire of available reform strategies. The program does three things: formulates new system-changing reform strategies that combine the strengths of existing proposals and avoid their weaknesses, offers assistance to local community leaders who must choose and implement reform strategies, and subjects contentious issues to rigorous examination in order to remove them from the realm of ideological conflict.

Program Plan

Brookings has committed itself to a program that will bring all the available ideas fully to bear on the problems of urban education. It hopes to provide an institutional home for collaboration among reform theorists, scholars, community leaders, and educators. The program's goals will be to provide advice and assistance to city leaders searching for effective reform strategies and to create a national agenda for development, trials, and evaluation of prospective reforms. In order to accomplish these goals the program will:

—Create a new menu of reform strategies that incorporates the strengths of reform theories now in competition with each other;

—Provide evidence to resolve ideological conflicts that prevent collaboration and retard public acceptance of strong reform strategies; and

—Create mechanisms of collaboration among reformers who now consider themselves rivals.

Creating a New Menu of Whole-System Reform Strategies

Despite the fact that no reform proposal has a corner on truth, it is clear that many proposals have a piece of it. Reformers from different schools of thought need to work together toward a richer mix of reform strategies than is available today, one that exploits the strengths of competing proposals but is not constrained by any of them. The program will develop new reform strategies via field research and simulation exercises. It will also try to weaken unwarranted opposition to promising reform initiatives via research on hot button issues such as those described in chapter 4.[1]

Field research will be conducted in cities that have created system-wide reform strategies that either combine key features of previously separate reforms or incorporate wholly new ideas. Brookings researchers will develop comparable case studies of five to ten such cities that have attempted integrated strategies of education reform. These case studies will become the data source for a cross-city analysis of the ways in which reform elements are combined into broader strategies and of how such reforms are formulated and implemented. A series of Brookings reports will help local leaders understand what has been attempted in other cities, identify possible implementation problems and how they might be overcome, and judge whether particular initiatives have yet shown any effect on schools and students. In each city the study will

—Identify districtwide reform strategies that combine elements of several different reform ideas.

—Explain the theories of action behind the combined reform strategies (in other words, show how the elements of the strategy are expected to work together to improve teaching and learning).

—Analyze the leadership and bargaining processes through which the combined reform strategies were created and the arrangements (including involvement of private organizations) through which the reform strategy is to be implemented and sustained beyond the tenure of an individual superintendent.

—Describe any arrangements made to track progress of reform implementation, to monitor whether the reform is progressing as the theory of action assumes, and to assess its effects on schools and students.

—Identify political, financial, and practical obstacles encountered in reform implementation to date and show how these were overcome.

Initial sites will be Seattle, San Francisco, Chicago, Boston, Memphis, New York City Community District Number 2, and San Antonio. Other cities will be studied throughout the life of the program. The first results of this work will be available in early 1999, in a Brookings book.

Simulation exercises allow reform innovators from different schools of thought to work together formulating new hybrid reform strategies for hypothetical cities. Such simulations create neutral forums in which people from different points of view and bases of experience can work together. They also allow people who represent particular interest groups (such as teachers' unions) to discuss possibilities that, in their everyday roles in their own communities, they could not openly consider. The Brookings project team will sponsor many such simulations across the country, and a diverse group of reformers from different schools of thought will analyze results to identify promising reform ideas that emerge.

Appendix A contains materials on how the simulations are conducted.

Resolving Hot Button Issues

Research on hot button issues will attempt to remove contentious issues from the realm of ideological conflict and to subject them to rigorous examination. Issues to be examined include the consequences of teacher-developed instructional methods, family choice, school competition, and more open teacher labor markets.

Brookings will convene panels of experts—including people who have research findings that bear on the problem and more general experts in analysis—to identify unresolved questions and areas of consensus. This effort will produce review articles on the status of research and clinical evidence, and it will formulate agendas for federally and foundation-sponsored research, trials, and demonstrations.

We will approach these questions through the consensus-conference method, as pioneered by the National Institutes of Health. Consensus conferences assemble experts who have evidence and opinions on important issues of medical practice and conduct a public review of the evidence, its validity and limitations, and the congruence between large-database studies and smaller clinical trials. A jury of clinical and methodological experts hears the evidence and identifies areas where consensus is strong, where disagreements can be reduced to matters of taste, and where data are so unsatisfactory as to require new or more rigorous examination. The results typically affect both clinical practice and national research and development priorities.

The topic of the first consensus panel, to be held in late 1998, will be the effects of family choice among schools on equality of opportunity. Possible topics for future conferences might include

—Under what circumstances do standards and high-stakes testing enrich or impoverish instruction?

—What is the evidence for retraining current teachers rather than seeking to change the teacher supply via different recruitment and preservice education?

—What is the evidence for and against the effectiveness of teacher-developed instructional methods?

—Under what conditions might a reform that promotes diverse approaches to schooling lead to creation of schools with separatist or divisive educational agendas?

Offering Help to Communities in Need

In addition to reports on field research results, Brookings will provide information about new reform strategies available to city leaders in several ways: national and regional meetings on lessons in urban reform; a publication series targeted to state and local lay leaders and elected officials; and an advice-brokering service that matches localities in need with groups of experts who have taken part in the development and testing of whole-system reform strategies, discussed above. Brookings will also publish books and articles for the informed public and elected officials about the legislative, funding, and implementation issues raised by new reform concepts.

Conclusion

These program plans extend only through the year 2000, but Brookings is permanently committed to urban education reform. When the current program is completed, Brookings hopes to help city leaders monitor and refine the reform strategies initiated in the next three years.

Materials for Simulation of Education Reform Strategy Building

SARA TAGGART

The Crisis

In June 2001, for the fourth year in a row, the performance of Edgeport schools on state assessments in fourth, eighth, and eleventh grade reading, writing, and math was disastrous. Last week (January 2002), following new guidelines for reconstitution, the state began taking action to shut down the district, dismiss the school board, and replace all principals and teachers with persons selected by the Office of the State Chief of Schools. In an impassioned plea, the mayor of Edgeport and the school board chair asked the state to reconsider.

The state chief of schools agreed to give the mayor's office and the school board two weeks to develop a comprehensive strategy for turning around the district. The chief of schools articulated one nonnegotiable goal:

> By spring 2003, every school in the district must have increased the proportion of students at grade level by 10 percent (relative to 2001 scores).

Office of the Mayor
City of Edgeport
500 West City Way
Edgeport

January 12, 2002

Dear —:

Thank you for agreeing to take part in the upcoming Blue Ribbon Panel on education reform. The panel will take place on Thursday, January 15, from 5:30–7:30 pm in Room 342, South Campus Center, at the University of Washington. Dinner will be provided and directions are enclosed.

As Mayor of the City of Edgeport, I am deeply, deeply concerned by the current crisis facing our city's schools. The situation is dire despite years of reform efforts. For the fourth year in a row, Edgeport students performed far below the state average on assessments in reading, writing and math. Last week, the State Chief of Schools informed me that the Edgeport School District will be taken over by the state. All current principals, teachers and other employees can be replaced by state-selected personnel. From then on, the education of our city's children will be out of our immediate control.

For the moment, Jack Figueras, Superintendent of Edgeport Schools, Francine Kraus, School Board Chair, and I have temporarily stalled the takeover. In two weeks we must submit for approval by the State Chief of Schools a comprehensive strategy to dramatically improve our schools by June 2003, just over one and a half years from now. With little time to spare, we need your help in devising a workable plan.

As a member of the Blue Ribbon Panel, you will advise us in our development of a reform strategy. We must act now; state control of our schools is not a viable option for our city's children! The panel will consist of four to six participants with expertise in education, school reform and other relevant areas. At the end of deliberations, I will ask the group to present your top three strategy recommendations. I will then share your recommendations with the Superintendent and School Board.

With your help, we can save Edgeport's schools. Radical, out-of-the-box thinking is needed to confront the challenges at hand. I look forward to hearing your ideas on this important matter.

Sincerely yours,

Angela O'Brien
Mayor

Timeline of Events

March 1997
New state learning standards are approved for fourth, eighth, and eleventh grades. The legislature instructs the state chief of schools to pilot the assessments in the spring of 1998.

June 1998
First round of assessments are administered. Edgeport results: all schools performed well below the state average in each area (reading, writing, and math). Ninety percent of schools averaged below comparison schools with similar student demographics in other districts. The school board resolves to reduce class size to 23:1 in all elementary grades, but no additional funding is approved to pay for staffing increases and space renovations.

June 1999
For the second year in a row, none of Edgeport's schools perform at or above state average. Ten percent of schools in the district show some improvement in reading and writing; 8 percent improve in math.

June 2000
No significant gains are registered in reading, writing, or math across the district. Public meetings are held to discuss the results and to solicit suggestions for school system improvements. Parents overwhelmingly emphasize the need to make schools safer and to make sure students learn basic skills that will help them get jobs. The Edgeport school board agrees to assess the language and writing curricula and to allocate more funds for campus security at four of the city's roughest high schools. The state chief of schools communicates that the Edgeport school district is being placed on probation with the possibility of being taken over by the state if next year's scores do not improve.

October 2000
Edgeport superintendent resigns in the midst of controversy over his leadership abilities. Districtwide curriculum development efforts stall. Schools with site-based decisionmaking councils fight against the recentralization of curricular decisionmaking.

March 2001
Lengthy search for new superintendent finally ends. Jack Figueras, superintendent of a coastal city in a neighboring state, is hired.

June 2001
State assessment results are made public. For the fourth year in a row the Edgeport school district fails to show any significant improvements.

November 2001
The Edgeport superintendent and school board chair receive notice that the district will be taken over by the state chief of schools office.

December 2001
The mayor, the superintendent, and the school board chair deliver a plea to the state chief of schools to allow them "a chance to prove themselves under the very new leadership of Jack Figueras."

January 5, 2002
After significant controversy, the chief of schools agrees to give the mayor's office and school board two weeks to develop a comprehensive strategy for how they will turn the district around, under the condition that the strategy must result in a 10 percent improvement in the proportion of students at grade level at each school. The mayor, the superintendent, and the board chair agree to convene a blue ribbon panel to advise them on reform strategies.

January 6, 2002
The mayor, the superintendent, and the board chair meet to discuss the crisis at hand. The following is a transcript of their meeting:

Mayor Angela O'Brien: We have to get a grip on the problem here in Edgeport. I am not going to be the mayor who let our schools get taken over by the state. Besides, when the state took over our twin city across the state, they made things worse and then dumped the problem back into the mayor's lap. State takeover is a threat to our city, not an option!

Board Chair Francine Kraus: I hear you, Angela, but we have to be realistic. Most of our students are poor and do not speak English at home.

Our teachers are ill equipped to deal with changing demographics and the new standards set by the state.

Superintendent Jack Figueras: Barriers or not, we have to do something drastic or else give up all control of our schools. I have compiled some information so we know what we're working with:

Edgeport District Profile, 2001–2002
— Urban district with 130 schools
— 58,000 students in K–12
— Student population is 35 percent Caucasian; 19 percent Asian; 26 percent Black; 2 percent Native American; 18 percent Hispanic.
— 53 percent of students are eligible to receive free or reduced price lunches
— 41 percent of students live in homes where English is not the primary language

Previous Reform Efforts
— 1970s: Efforts focused on districtwide curricular revisions and teacher retraining. Most teachers have abandoned these methods in the face of changing student demographics and new state standards.
— Small and vocal group of middle-class parents pushed for the development of fifteen alternative schools with unique programs. The district had hoped that the success of these schools would inspire other schools to improve. There is no evidence of this kind of impact.
— Two-thirds of the schools have operating school site councils as a result of decentralization efforts. These schools have greater control over curricula and budget decisions than their counterparts. They do not control hiring decisions.
— State legislators are proposing a state-funded voucher program, which would allow the lowest-income 10 percent of public school students to enter a voucher lottery to fill vacant seats in local private and religious schools. There are 900 vacancies in existing private schools.
— A separate charter school bill, which appears likely to pass within one year would allow creation of five new schools in the district each year.

Kraus: Clearly we need a plan that builds on our strengths. And another thing, we can't forget that the teachers' union will likely be on our side. State takeover cancels all job rights.

O'Brien: Has the state given us any word as to whether or not it will provide extra funding if we present a viable plan?

Figueras: The state will not provide extra finances yet, but the Office of the State Chief of Schools will provide technical assistance. And any kind of levy funding is out of the question before our deadline, June 2003.

Kraus: I recommend that we meet on next Friday, January 16, ready to formulate our strategy. In the meantime, Angela will hear from the blue ribbon panel and can bring their recommendations to the table as well.

AGENDA

Please help yourself to dinner as you arrive.

Welcome, review agenda, introductions
    Sara Taggart, Mayor's Office
    Larry Pierce, Facilitator
	5:30 pm

Presentation on recent school reform research Paul Hill, Brookings Institution	5:50 pm

Blue Ribbon Panel deliberations
    Panel deliberates and comes to consensus
    on recommendations
	6:00 pm

Panel presentation, Q & A
    Panel presents top three strategy
    recommendations to Mayor O'Brien
	7:00 pm

Debrief of simulation activity	7:15 pm
Closing	7:30 pm

To: Mayor Angela O'Brien
From: Staff Working Group
Re: Bold School Reform Options

DRAFT MEMORANDUM

As requested, here are several options that meet your "strong medicine" criterion. We do not necessarily endorse these, but think they represent the kind of "out of the box" thinking you requested.

1.   Provide massive retraining for the 25 percent of all teachers whose students scored lowest on the city tests.

2.   Give any student enrolled in the bottom 10 percent of schools first priority to transfer to any public school in the city.

3.   Establish five new charter schools (three elementary, one middle, one high) to compete with the five lowest-performing schools in the district.

4.   Set up a lump-sum budgeting system giving school principals control of 90 percent of all dollars, plus staff hiring and firing.

5.   Seek special funding to bring in whole-school design teams such as New American Schools or Edison to lead transformation of schools scoring in the lowest quartile.

6.   If scores in the bottom-quartile schools do not improve within two years, give vouchers to parents of all children in those schools, allowing them to transfer out of the district or to private schools.

7.   Reassign principals and teachers from the highest-performing schools so that all local schools have at least one "exemplary teacher."

8.   Convert three lowest-performing high schools into alternative schools with emphasis on vocational training and work force preparation. Give lowest-performing students priority in admissions.

Sources B

In addition to interviews, the study was informed by review of the following sources:

Bay Area School Reform Collaborative (Hewlett-Annenberg Challenge Grant). "Member and Leadership School Activities for the 1996–97 School Year," mimeographed guidelines, 1996.

Bimber, Bruce A. 1993. *School Decentralization: Lessons from the Study of Bureaucracy* (Santa Monica, Calif.: RAND).

———. 1994. *The Decentralization Mirage: Comparing Arrangements in Four High Schools* (Santa Monica, Calif.: RAND).

Bodilly, Susan, and others. 1995. *Designing New American Schools: Baseline Observations on Nine Design Teams* (Santa Monica, Calif.: RAND).

Chubb, John E., and Eric A. Hanushek. 1990. "Reforming Educational Reform." In *Setting National Priorities: Policy for the Nineties,* edited by Henry J. Aaron, 213–48 (Brookings).

Chubb, John E., and Terry M. Moe. 1990. *Politics, Markets, and America's Schools* (Brookings).

Clune, William H., and John F. Witte, eds. 1990. *Choice and Control in American Education,* Stanford series on education and public policy, 2 vols. (Bristol, Pa: Falmer Press).

Coons, John E. 1985. "Intellectual Liberty and the Schools." *Journal of Law, Ethics and Public Policy* 1: 495–533.

———. 1992. "School Choice and Simple Justice." *First Things,* vol. 22 (April): 15–22.

Glennan, Thomas K., Jr. 1998. *New American Schools after Six Years* (Santa Monica, Calif.: RAND).

Hirsch, E. D., Jr. 1996. *The Schools We Need and Why We Don't Have Them* (New York: Doubleday).

Kearns, David T., and Denis P. Doyle. 1991. *Winning the Brain Race: A Bold Plan to Make Our Schools Competitive* (San Francisco: ICS Press).

Millot, Marc Dean, with Robin Lake. 1996. *Creating a Market for Public Schools: Lessons Learned from Early Implementation of the Massachusetts Charter School Statute* (Washington, D.C., and Seattle, Wash.: RAND Institute for Education and Training and the University of Washington Program for Reinventing Public Education).

New American Schools. 1996. *Working toward Excellence: Early Indicators from Schools Implementing New American Schools Designs* (Arlington, Va.: New American Schools).

Ravitch, Diane. 1995. *National Standards in American Education: A Citizen's Guide.* Brookings.

Notes

Chapter One

1. There is a raging debate about whether school outcomes have improved overall and especially for the urban poor. David C. Berliner and Bruce J. Biddle, *The Manufactured Crisis: Myths, Fraud, and the Attack on America's Public Schools* (Reading, Mass.: Addison-Wesley, 1995), and David W. Grissmer and others, *Student Achievement and the Changing American Family* (Santa Monica, Calif.: RAND, 1994), provide some evidence that average test scores for minority students have risen slightly in the past generation, but none provides evidence that the gap between minority and majority students is likely to close in the foreseeable future. On the contrary, data from the National Assessment of Educational Progress and the SATs indicate that the one–standard deviation difference between mean white and black scores has persisted over time and is not narrowing appreciably. Overall performance of U.S. students is also stable relative to scores from other countries. Studies of educational practices and school quality reinforce the view that public education, especially in big cities, is not improving. Measures of teacher quality, time spent on instruction, student failure rate, student and teacher attendance, and content coverage in classes are all stable or declining. Internally driven reform efforts are also highly unstable and seldom reach beyond the small cadres of enthusiasts who have a taste for reform and experimentation. Richard F. Elmore, "Getting to Scale with Good Educational Practice," *Harvard Educational Review*, vol. 66, no. 1 (Spring 1996), pp. 1–26; also Donna E. Muncey and Patrick J. McQuillan, *Reform and Resistance in Schools and Classrooms: An Ethnographic View of the Coalition of Essential Schools* (Yale University Press, 1996); and Paul T. Hill, Lawrence Pierce, and James W. Guthrie, *Reinventing*

Public Education: How Contracting Can Transform America's Schools (University of Chicago Press, 1997).

2. David A. Bostitis, *Joint Center for Political and Economic Studies 1997 Opinion Poll—Children's Issues* (Washington, D.C.: Center on Political and Economic Studies, 1998).

3. John E. Chubb and Terry M. Moe, *Politics, Markets, and America's Schools* (Brookings, 1990).

Chapter Two

1. For a list of sources consulted (in addition to the interviews), see appendix B.

2. Richard F. Elmore, "Getting to Scale with Good Educational Practice," *Harvard Educational Review*, vol. 66, no. 1 (Spring 1996), pp. 1–26.

3. We assume here that the goal of all reforms discussed in this book is that students gain the skills and knowledge they need as adults in our society. Some reformers do not accept this as the only, or even primary, goal, opting instead for "building community," "encouraging diversity," "honoring multiple intelligences," or even "keeping kids safe." John Witte, in his introduction to volume 1 of *Choice and Control in American Education*, even goes so far as to see a "prominent and prevalent clash" over the value placed on raising educational achievement versus fostering greater equity in achievement (p. 9). However, academic achievement is always included as a goal by school theorists and reformers, even if it is only one of many worthy goals. William H. Clune and John F. Witte, eds., *Choice and Control in American Education*, Stanford Series on Education and Public Policy (Bristol, Pa.: Falmer Press, 1990).

4. For a full exposition, see Paul T. Hill, Lawrence Pierce, and James Guthrie, *Reinventing Public Education: How Contracting Can Transform America's Schools* (University of Chicago Press, 1997).

5. For an extensive comparison of the cause-and-effect assumptions made by vouchers, charters, and contracting, see Hill, Pierce, and Guthrie, *Reinventing Public Education*, chapter 4.

6. See, for example, Anthony S. Bryk, David Kerbow, and Sharon Rollow, "Chicago School Reform," in Diane Ravitch and Joseph Vitiretti, eds., *New Schools for a New Century* (Yale University Press, 1997).

7. In fact, the strongest criticism of the standards movement is that it threatens to add to the chaos and disunity in schools by imposing such exacting requirements in different areas that schools must choose whether to meet some but not others or to fall short on all of them.

8. In the three cities, schools must meet a universal set of student achievement standards but are encouraged to adopt distinctive approaches to teaching. Many individual schools in Cincinnati have adopted designs developed by New American Schools. These efforts have just begun and it is too early to report on the results. Brookings city case studies, described in chapter 6, will produce reports on at least two of these efforts to combine standards and school designs.

9. See, for example, Paul T. Hill, *How to Create Incentives for Design-Based Schools* (Arlington, Va.: New American Schools, 1997). See also Allan Odden, *How to Rethink*

School Budgets to Support School Transformation (Arlington, Va.: New American Schools, 1997). http://www.naschools.org/resource/howto/oddenbud.pdf.

Chapter Three

1. See, for example, John E. Chubb and Terry M. Moe, *Politics, Markets, and America's Schools* (Brookings, 1990); Jonathan Kozol, *Savage Inequalities: Children in America's Schools* (Harper Perennial, 1992); Paul T. Hill, Gail E. Foster, and Tamar Gendler, *High Schools with Character* (Santa Monica, Calif.: RAND, 1990); Arthur G. Powell, Eleanor Farrar, and David K. Cohen, *The Shopping Mall High School: Winners and Losers in the Educational Marketplace* (Boston: Houghton Mifflin, 1985); Anthony S. Bryk and others, *Catholic Schools and the Common Good* (Harvard University Press, 1993).

2. See, for example, Valerie E. Lee, Julia B. Smith, and Robert G. Croninger, "How High School Organization Influences the Equitable Distribution of Learning in Mathematics and Science," *Sociology of Education*, vol. 70, no. 2 (April 1997), pp.128–50; Deborah Meier, *The Power of Their Ideas: Lessons for America from a Small School in Harlem* (Boston: Beacon Press, 1995); Bryk and others, *Catholic Schools and the Common Good*; Jacqueline Jordan Irvine and Michele Foster, eds., *Growing Up African American in Catholic Schools* (New York: Teachers College Press, 1996); Susan J. Rosenholtz, *Teachers' Workplace: The Social Organization of Schools* (New York: Longman, 1989); Ronald Edmonds, *A Discussion of the Literature and Issues Related to Effective Schooling* (St. Louis: CEMREL, 1979); Jeannie Oakes, *Keeping Track: How Schools Structure Inequality* (Yale University Press, 1985); James S. Coleman and Thomas Hoffer, *Public and Private High Schools: The Impact of Communities* (New York: Basic Books, 1987); Charles Teddie and Sam Stringfield, *Schools Make a Difference: Lessons Learned from a Ten-Year Study of School Effects* (New York: Teachers College Press, 1993); Hill, Foster, and Gendler, *High Schools with Character*; Paul T. Hill, "The Educational Consequences of Choice," *Phi Delta Kappan* (1995); Herbert J. Walberg, "Uncompetitive American Schools: Causes and Cures," *Brookings Papers on Education Policy: 1998*.

3. All these factors have been shown at one time or other to correlate with student achievement, as have other even more microscopic characteristics of schools (class size, teacher qualifications, availability of books and instructional materials, and per-pupil funding). However, no one of these factors is enough by itself to increase student achievement, so that it is possible for any of the factors to be present in a low-performing school. How to create schools that combine all the apparently important factors and are able to maintain themselves against threats posed by regulatory change, staff turnover, and other external pressures is the fundamental unsolved problem of public education.

4. See, for example, Tom Loveless, "The Use and Misuse of Research in Education Reform," *Brookings Papers on Education Policy: 1998*. Loveless contends that many of the factors identified by research as correlated with high rates of student learning are incorporated into laws and policies without sufficient thought. In the process, findings about individual attributes of effective schools are "disconnected from a base of substantiating evidence, thereby distorting what research actually recommends" (p. 285). Loveless holds that lists of discrete school attributes, especially those founded on the 1970s "effective

schools literature" (such as Edmonds, *A Discussion of the Literature and Issues Related to Effective Schooling*) neglected key steps in the educational system, thus severely limiting the usefulness of the findings from these studies.

5. Paul T. Hill and others, *Schools' Integrative Capital,* Working papers of the University of Washington Graduate School of Public Affairs, 1998.

6. The concept of integrative capital draws from many sources, including the work of Fred M. Newmann and others, *Authentic Achievement: Restructuring Schools for Intellectual Quality* (San Francisco: Jossey-Bass, 1996); Valerie E. Lee and Julia B. Smith, *Effects of High School Restructurinng and Size on Gains in Achievement and Engagement for Early Secondary School Students* (Madison, Wis.: Center on Organization and Restructuring of Schools, 1996); Anthony S. Bryk, Valerie E. Lee and Peter Blakeley Holland, *Catholic Schools and the Common Good* (Harvard University Press, 1993); Edmonds, *A Discussion of the Literature and Issues Related to Effective Schooling;* and Hill, Foster, and Gendler, *High Schools with Character.* It goes beyond the "effective schools" literature, which lists attributes of productive schools but does not explain how they come about or are sustained. It is consistent with Newmann's work on schools' organizational capacity, which he defines as a school's ability to "organize itself as a collective enterprise, uniting the use of human, social, and technical resources." (Fred M. Newmann and Gary C. Wehlage, *Successful School Restructuring* [Madison, Wis.: Center on Organization and Restructuring of Schools, 1995], pp. 29–30.) Integrative capital looks beneath the phenomenon of collaboration to the ideas about teaching and learning that underlay it. The concept of integrative capital, in short, sees leadership, shared commitment, and collaboration as results of something deeper—goals for students and a strategy of teaching and learning that can help students reach those goals.

7. Research on the characteristics and effects of magnet schools may be of some help here, if only because such schools are found in virtually all major urban school systems and have been researched at several points in their history. Although often begun as part of desegregation efforts, one of the primary characteristics of such schools is that they offer "a special curricular theme or method of instruction." Rolf K. Blank, "Educational Effects of Magnet High Schools," in William H. Clune and John F. Witte, eds., *Choice and Control in American Education,* vol. 2: *The Practice of Choice, Decentralization, and School Restructuring* (Bristol, Pa.: Falmer Press, 1990), reported that a 1983 national study showed that three magnet school policy and organization variables were significantly related to quality of education process and outcomes: "(a) principal leadership; (b) coherence between the magnet theme and the curriculum and staffing; and (c) district policy commitment and flexibility with proceedings."

8. See, for example, John E. Chubb and Terry M. Moe, "Politics, Markets, and the Organization of Schools," *American Political Science Review,* vol. 88 (December 1988).

9. Cecelia-Elena Rouse, "Schools and Student Achievement: More Evidence from the Milwaukee Parental Choice Program," *Federal Reserve Bank of New York Economic Policy Review,* vol. 4 (March): 61–76.

10. Paul T. Hill, Lawrence Pierce, and James Guthrie, *Reinventing Public Education: How Contracting Can Transform America's Schools* (University of Chicago Press, 1997).

11. John E. Chubb and Terry M. Moe, *Politics, Markets, and America's Schools* (Brookings, 1990).

12. John I. Goodlad, "Democracy, Education, and Community," in Roger Soder, ed., *Democracy, Education, and the Schools* (San Francisco: Jossey-Bass, 1996); and David C. Berliner, "Educational Psychology Meets the Christian Right: Differing Views of Children, Schooling, Teaching, and Learning," *Teachers College Record*, vol. 98 (Spring), pp. 381–416.

13. Bruce Fuller, Richard Elmore, and Gary Orfield, *School Choice: The Cultural Logic of Families, the Political Rationality of Institutions* (New York: Teachers College Press, 1996).

14. See Dorothy Shipps, "Big Business and School Reform: The Case of Chicago 1988," Ph.D. dissertation, Stanford University School of Education, 1995.

15. The claim that minority hiring is essential to educational quality in big cities— that only minority teachers can connect with minority students—remains in dispute. On the theme that minority teachers are not necessarily indispensable to the education of minority children, see Ronald Ferguson, "Racial Patterns in How School and Teacher Quality Affect Achievement and Earnings," *Challenge*, vol. 2, no. 1 (May 1991), pp. 1–35. However, a contrary argument is made by Linda Darling-Hammond, "What Matters Most: A Competent Teacher for Every Child," *Phi Delta Kappan*, vol. 78, no. 3 (November 1996), pp. 193–200.

16. On threats to central office employment, see Paul T. Hill, *How to Create Incentives for Design-Based Schools* (Arlington, Va.: New American Schools, 1997).

17. See, for example, Marc S. Tucker and Judy B. Codding, *Standards for Our Schools: How to Set Them, Measure Them, and Reach Them* (San Francisco: Jossey-Bass, 1998), chapter 6.

18. For a review of legal and political issues associated with major reform proposals, see Hill, Pierce, and Guthrie, *Reinventing Public Education*, chapter 7.

19. A similar process has caused raw conflict between parents for and against charter schools in some Massachusetts towns. See Marc Dean Millot and Robin Lake, "Supplying a System of Charter Schools: Observations on Early Implementation of the Massachusetts Statute" (University of Washington Center on Reinventing Public Education, 1997).

20. See Allan Odden, "Decentralized Management and School Finance," *Theory into Practice*, vol. 33, no. 2 (Spring 1994), pp.104–11.

21. See, for example, Sari Horwitz, "Poll Finds Backing for D.C. School Vouchers; Blacks Support Idea More Than Whites, *Washington Post*, May 23, 1998, p. F1. See also Jean Johnson and John Immerwahr, "First Things First: What Americans Expect from the Public Schools," *American Educator*, vol. 18, no. 4 (Winter 1995), pp. 4–6, 8, 11–13, 44–45.

22. Janet A. Weiss, "Control in School Organizations: Theoretical Perspectives," in Clune and Witte, eds., *Choice and Control in American Education*, vol. 1, pp. 91–133.

23. Walberg, "Uncompetitive American Schools." Walberg cites research by Caroline Minter Hoxby and Sam Peltzman showing that union success has been associated with growth of per-student costs, and drop-out rates, and falling test scores in the forty-eight states they studied. Caroline Minter Hoxby, "How Teachers' Unions Affect Education Production," *Quarterly Journal of Economics*, vol. 3, no. 3 (August 1996), pp. 671–718; and Sam Peltzman, "Political Economy of Public Education: Non-College-Bound Students," *Journal of Law and Economics*, vol. 39 (April 1996), pp. 73–120.

Chapter 4

1. David C. Berliner, "Educational Psychology Meets the Christian Right: Differing Views of Children, Schooling, Teaching, and Learning," *Teachers College Record*, vol. 98 (Spring, 1997): 381–416.

2. Ibid.

3. Our explanation of these issues is itself a product of preliminary research, sponsored by Brookings and the Spencer Foundation, on the roots of controversy over public school reform. Many of the issues presented in this chapter were formulated in the course of a workshop on "hot buttons" held at Brookings in October 1997. Participants were Bruce Fuller, University of California, Berkeley; Paul Hill, Brookings; Lorraine McDonnell, University of California, Santa Barbara; Joseph Murphy, Vanderbilt University; Robert Schwartz, Harvard University; and Carol Weiss, Harvard University. Others commenting on the results include Mary Beth Celio and Lawrence Pierce of the University of Washington and Cecilia Rouse of Princeton University.

4. See, for example, Alex Molnar, *Smaller Classes, Not Vouchers, Increase Student Achievement* (Harrisburg, Pa.: Keystone Research Center, 1998), p. 25.

5. Sebring and Bryk's studies of school reform in Chicago validate both points of view. See Penny Bender Sebring and others, *Charting Reform: Chicago Teachers Take Stock* (Consortium on Chicago School Research, 1995), http://www.consortium-chicago.org/html_web_store_3.0/html/takestock_desc.html. As Sebring and Bryk report, approximately one-fourth of the elementary schools in Chicago improved under a deliberation-based reform, half the schools did not change, and about one-fourth of the schools got much worse. They speculate that deliberation can work well in schools where families and teachers trust in one another's basic values, but that it cannot create a good school in deeply split communities.

6. For representative literature on both sides of this issue, see Amy Gutmann and Dennis Thompson, *Democracy and Disagreement* (Cambridge, Mass.: Belknap Press, 1996); Michael S. Joyce and William A. Schambra, "A New Civic Life," in Michael Novak, *To Empower People: From State to Civil Society* (Washington, D.C.: American Enterprise Institute, 1996), http://www.aei.org/3944-8.pdf; and James M. Buchanan and Gordon Tullock, *The Calculus of Consent* (University of Michigan Press, 1962).

7. As chapter 6 explains, Brookings will initiate a serious data search and consensus-building process on these questions.

8. For an excellent discussion, see John R. Anderson, Lynne M. Reder, and Herbert A. Simon, "Radical Constructivism and Cognitive Psychology," *Brookings Papers on Education Policy: 1998*. See also comments by K. Anders Ericsson and Robert Glaser. For an example of misplaced certitudes, pro and con modern instructional methods, see Berliner, "Educational Psychology Meets the Christian Right."

9. U.S. Department of Education, Office of Educational Research and Improvement, *A Study of Charter Schools: First-Year Report, 1997* (RPP International and the University of Minnesota), http://www.ed.gov/pubs/charter; and Gregg Vanourek and others, "Charter Schools as Seen by Those Who Know Them Best: Students, Teachers, and Parents," *Charter Schools in Action, A Hudson Institute Project* (Indianapolis: Hudson Institute, 1997).

10. People differ on whether education for democracy also requires attending school in the company of a diverse group of students, representative of the all the races, income

groups, and ways of thinking present in the broader community. There are three arguments against the necessity of student body diversity. First, schools constrained to serve extremely diverse populations are often ineffective because they cannot be highly focused and coherent in their instructional methods. Second, schools that serve highly diverse groups can seldom create the experience of integrated schooling because of differences in students' preferences and preparation; many nominally integrated schools are diverse only in a statistical sense, and most students' experience is with students very much like themselves. Third, differences in race, income, and values often make deliberation difficult and emotionally charged, so that students in highly diverse schools learn to avoid difficult topics (or to stick to politically correct formulas) rather than to discuss important issues earnestly; in contrast, students in more cohesive schools defined by certain shared values often debate vigorously. Others dispute the evidence for these points and present as examples schools that model successful deliberation among highly diverse groups of students. They argue that habits of deliberation must be learned early and that grouping students in ways to make deliberation easy ill-suit them for the more diverse world in which they will live.

11. See, for example, Paul T. Hill, "The Educational Consequences of Choice," *Phi Delta Kappan*, vol. 77, no. 10 (June 1996), pp. 671–75.

12. Many of the ideas presented here were developed in the course of a Spencer Foundation workshop on choice and democracy in education held at the University of Washington in April 1996. Participants included Rabbi Bernard Fox of the Northwest Yeshiva, Pamela Grossman of the University of Washington, Paul Hill of the University of Washington, Lorraine McDonnell of the University of California, Santa Barbara, David Paris of Hamilton College, Vance Randall of Brigham Young University, Diane Ravitch of the Brookings Institution, Andrea Sledge of Seattle University, and David Steiner of Vanderbilt University.

13. See, for example, Amy Stewart Wells, *Time to Choose: America at the Crossroads of School Choice* (New York: Hill and Wang, 1993); Claire Smrekar, *The Impact of School Choice And Community: In the Interest of Families and Schools* (Albany: State University of New York Press, 1996); Jeffrey R. Henig, *Rethinking School Choice: Limits of the Market Metaphor* (Princeton University Press, 1994); Judith Pearson, *Myths of Educational Choice* (Westport, Conn.: Praeger, 1993); *School Choice: A Special Report* (Princeton, N.J.: The Carnegie Foundation for the Advancement of Teaching, 1992); Amy Stuart Wells, *Public School Choice: Issues and Concerns for Urban Educators* (New York: ERIC Clearinghouse on Urban Education); Bruce Fuller, *Who Gains, Who Loses from School Choice: A Research Summary* (Denver: National Conference of State Legislatures, 1995); and John Witte, *Choice in American Education: Policy Issues* (Charleston, W. Va.: Appalachia Educational Lab, 1990).

14. Bruce Fuller, Richard Elmore, and Gary Orfield, *Who Chooses? Who Loses? Culture, Institutions, and the Unequal Effects of School Choice* (New York: Teachers College Press, 1996).

15. Carol Ascher, Robert Berne, and Norman Fruchter, *Hard Lessons: Public Schools and Privatization* (New York: Twentieth Century Fund Press, 1996).

16. Smrekar, *The Impact of School Choice and Community*.

17. See, for example, Terry M. Moe's introductory chapter in his edited volume, *Private Vouchers* (Stanford, Calif.: Hoover Institution Press, 1995). See also Paul Hill, "Pri-

vate Vouchers in New York City: The Student-Sponsor Partnership Program," in Moe, *Private Vouchers.*

18. No less a commentator than Pope John Paul II has weighed into this area, commenting on a recent visit to Cuba, "It is true that in the area of education, public authority has certain rights and duties, since it must serve the common good. Nonetheless, this does not give public authority the right to take the place of parents. Consequently, parents, without expecting others to replace them in a matter which is their own responsibility, should be able to choose for their children the pedagogical method, the ethical and civic content and the religious inspiration which will enable them to receive an integral education. They must not expect everything to be given to them." "Pope's Words: Family and Responsibility," *New York Times,* January 23, 1998, p. A11.

19. We are indebted to Professor Lorraine McDonnell for suggesting this line of analysis.

Chapter 5

1. In search of new ideas about how cities can construct reform strategies, Brookings is constructing a series of simulated community decisionmaking processes. These simulations (described briefly in chapter 6 and in detail in appendix A) involve community leaders and education reform experts in a structured discussion about how to save the school system of a fictitious city from state takeover. The simulations serve two purposes: First, they familiarize participants with problems they may need to face in real life, in a safe and low-pressure environment that allows them to try out ideas and debate issues without committing themselves to public positions. Second, the simulations can produce new ideas that leaders operating under real-world political pressures and time constraints have not been able to develop.

2. Sources include Anthony S. Bryk and others, *Decentralization in Practice: Toward a System of Schools* (Consortium on Chicago School Research, 1997); and Paul T. Hill, Arthur E. Wise, and Leslie Shapiro, *Educational Progress: Cities Mobilize to Improve Their Schools* (Santa Monica, Calif.: RAND, 1989).

3. Outside education, RAND has provided critical friend services to local economic development initiatives in Cleveland and Pittsburgh. For descriptions of these forms of help and their results, see Aaron S. Gurwitz and G. Thomas Kingsley, *The Cleveland Metropolitan Economy* (Santa Monica, Calif.: RAND, 1982).

4. Charlotte, North Carolina, invited such a panel of national experts to help develop its reform strategy. The result—a set of student achievement standards backed up by annual performance agreements with each school that also created new sources of assistance tailored to each school's needs—was an unusually coherent and effective reform. Overall student test scores, and scores for African American students in particular, grew significantly. However, the superintendent's confrontational style soon led to political conflicts that eroded support for the reform, despite its positive effects on instruction and student achievement.

5. For an analysis of ways existing funds can be used more flexibly in support of a citywide reform strategy, see Allan Odden, *How to Rethink School Budgets to Support School Transformation* (Arlington, Va.: New American Schools, 1997). See also Allan

Odden, "Raising Performance Levels without Increasing Funding," *School Business Affairs*, vol. 63, no. 6 (June 1997), pp. 4–12.

6. For a discussion of stakeholder incentives and how to gain school system insiders' support for reform, see Paul T. Hill, *How to Create Incentives for Design-Based Schools* (Arlington, Va.: New American Schools, 1997), http://www.naschools.org/resource/howto/hill.pdf.

7. The term school design is shorthand for a school's integrative capital. From a recent New American Schools publication: "A school design is an architecture that guides the efforts of individual teachers to complement one another and shows how the school as a whole can work to ensure that students learn what they must know. A school design suggests:

• What information, skills, habits and values the school intends to impart to all students (and, implicitly, what forms of student learning does the school consider of secondary importance).

• How all the instructional and other experiences the school offers students complement one another to help students gain key knowledge, skills, and habits of mind;

• What effort and performance the school demands of students; and

• How the school motivates students, both by making learning intrinsically rewarding and demonstrating that meeting the school's demands leads to desirable outcomes for the students

• What repertoire of methods individual teachers will use in doing their jobs;

• How the work of different teachers is expected to fit together." Ibid.

8. For detailed discussions of New American Schools' ideas about school designs and NAS's capacities for school assistance, see Thomas K. Glennan, *New American Schools After Six Years* (Santa Monica, Calif.: RAND, 1998); and Hill, *How to Create Incentives for Design-Based Schools*.

9. These three essential features of a reform strategy are drawn from an earlier formulation suggested by Anthony Bryk. In the course of a study on school system decentralization, he suggested that a complete decentralization plan must have three As: autonomy, assistance, and accountability. Our categories of opportunity, capabilities, and incentives are closely related to Bryk's ideas, which are developed in Bryk and others, *Decentralization in Practice.*

10. Seattle's widely admired, school-based budgeting plan still allocates less than 50 percent of all funds to the schools, and it does not allow schools to trade in high-salaried senior teachers for greater numbers of lower-cost junior teachers. Seattle School District, *Weighted Student Formula: Budget Alloction to Schools for the 1997–1998 School Year* (Seattle Public Schools, 1997).

11. For a more complete exposition of this strategy, see Paul T. Hill, Lawrence Pierce, and James Guthrie, *Reinventing Public Education: How Contracting Can Transform America's Schools* (University of Chicago Press, 1997).

12. Anthony S. Bryk and others, *A View from the Elementary Schools: The State of Reform in Chicago* (Consortium on Chicago School Research, 1993).

13. For a union leader's promising vision of a future performance-oriented school system, see Adam Urbanski and Mary Beth Nickolaou, "Reflections on Teachers as Leaders," *Educational Policy*, vol. 11, no. 2 (June 1997), pp. 243–54.

Chapter 6

1. A collaborating institution, RAND, will seek funds separately to design strategies for demonstrations and controlled trials of promising reform proposals. It hopes to develop designs for local pilot programs that will subject particular reform proposals to fair and informative test. These designs will help state and local leaders understand what must be done in order to fully implement and test a reform strategy. They might also be used to encourage federal investment in rigorous trials of key reform proposals.

Index